Government
Regulation of
Higher Education

Government Regulation of Higher Education

Edited by:
Walter C. Hobbs
State University of New York at Buffalo

Ballinger Publishing Company ● **Cambridge, Massachusetts**
A Subsidiary of J.B. Lippincott Company

This book is printed on recycled paper.

International Standard Book Number: 0-88410-183-5

Library of Congress Catalog Card Number: 77-27442

Printed in the United States of America

Library of Congress Cataloging in Publication Data

Main entry under title:

Government regulation of higher education.

 Includes index.
 1. Higher education and state—United States—Addresses, essays, lectures. 2. Universities and colleges—United States—Administration—Addresses, essays, lectures. I. Hobbs, Walter C.
LC173.G74   379.73   77-27442
ISBN 0-88410-183-5

To
G. LESTER ANDERSON: scholar, administrator,
mentor, friend

Contents

✳

Preface

Government regulation is certainly no stranger to commerce
and industry, but only lately has it developed with great force
among colleges and universities. This book examines that
development from the perspectives of the legal scholar, the university
president, the university lawyer, the government lawyer, the university affirmative-action officer, the professional association's watch-dog
of government activity, and the statesman-scholar of higher education.

Each essay—and they are essays, not formal analyses—is at bottom
a value statement asserting what is good and what is bad in government regulation of academe. Some papers deal directly with the topic,
while others touch it only indirectly (especially Tobias and Wollett).
But all find in the regulatory phenomenon their point of contact with
one another, for each was solicited to contribute to—and to fuel—a
reasoned, if occasionally impassioned, debate of the title theme.

The papers are revised versions of presentations made to a conference on Horizon Issues in Government Regulation of Higher Education, convened in April 1977 by the Department of Higher Education at
the State University of New York at Buffalo. Many people play a
variety of roles in such an effort, but special recognition is due Marjorie
C. Mix, then faculty colleague in the department and currently staff
attorney with the New York State Office of Employee Relations, for her
invaluable collaboration in framing the substance of the conference
program, which became essentially the substance of this book.

The costs of the conference as well as the expense of preparing the manuscript for publication were underwritten by the Baldy Endowment of the State University of New York at Buffalo. And Ms. Pamela Morgan provided the usual necessary typing services, but with unusual competence and efficiency. I am indebted to both, for without their support the work would not have come to fruition.

WALTER C. HOBBS

Government
Regulation of
Higher Education

Chapter 1

The Theory of
Government Regulation

Walter C. Hobbs

It is commonplace to hear that in the past decade or so, law has
intruded on academic affairs—as if this were a recent development. The truth is that law has been "intruding" on academe
for centuries, often at the instance of academics themselves. Its operation today is only more noticeable and more noticed, not more powerful
or pervasive than before.

As early as 1243, canon lawyers resurrected the ancient Roman
doctrine of the fictitious corporate person, and Pope Innocent IV invested academic enterprises with corporate character—a thoroughly
legal concept.[1] Less than fifty years later, Emperor Frederick II challenged papal dominance in the field by issuing charters from the
Crown, and the first "state universities" were given life. The corporate
charter developed extensively in England during the fifteenth and
sixteenth centuries, finding application in a plethora of ventures beyond academe from municipalities to charities to trading companies.
And when in the seventeenth century the Pietists settled the Massachusetts Bay Colony, they almost immediately employed the device in
founding Harvard College. Moreover, to the monies supplied the new
school from private sources (one-half the estate of John Harvard and a
near-equivalent amount contributed collectively by others), "the pub-
lique hand of the State added the rest."[2]

What the sovereign provided—namely, legal existence and sus-
tenance—the sovereign could withdraw. At least, so thought the sovereign state of New Hampshire, on impeccably conclusive historical
evidence, until its quarrel with the trustees of Dartmouth College in
1817. For reasons that need not detain us here, the legislature had

increased the number of trustees established by the college's charter of 1769, had filled the additional positions with persons of their own choosing, and had created a Board of Overseers enjoying veto power over the actions of the trustees. But the U.S. Supreme Court held that a corporate charter is not subject to legislative modification or repeal simply because it is granted by the state, that the charter is instead a contract between the state and the corporation's trustees that is protected by the federal Constitution against impairment by state law.[3] Before the U.S. Constitution had reached the age of thirty, law had again "intruded," first legislatively, then judicially, in academe.

The *Dartmouth* case understandably gave pause to legislatures that previously had appropriated public funds to the colleges they had chartered. The power of the sovereign over its corporate creations was now severely circumscribed, and two-thirds of a century were yet to pass before the alternative device of the regulatory commission would come into its own. Public funding of higher education all but ceased; the era of the private college had dawned.[4]

Therein perhaps is found the roots of today's misimpression that law's impact on academic affairs is a relatively new phenomenon. To be sure, *Dartmouth* placed unexpected limits on the power of government vis-à-vis institutional boards of control. And both government and academe responded predictably, given the nature of their respective interests: government withdrew much of its support and oversight, and higher education began to steer a new course through the choppy waters of private philanthropy. But it is simply not the case that government and higher education bid one another adieu in the early 1800s, to meet again a century and a quarter later. Both case law and statute continued to play important roles in shaping academe.

Item. In 1850, a New York court entertained a suit by villagers of the town of Hamilton to prevent removal of Colgate University to the city of Rochester. The villagers won,[5] and the Baptist Education Society of New York founded instead the University of Rochester.[6]

Item. In 1862, the Morrill Act was adopted by the Congress, authorizing the federal provision of resources by which states might establish publicly supported, publicly governed, "land-grant" universities and colleges. Together with the Hatch Act of 1887, which authorized the funding of research and experiment stations, and the Smith-Lever Act of 1914, which authorized support to "extension" programs in agriculture and home economics, the Morrill Act of 1862 (and its supplemental counterparts of 1890 and 1907) produced one of history's most remarkable cooperative arrangements between government and academe.

Item. In 1866, an Illinois court found "inherent power" in a college to discipline students as a proper means to maintain scholastic standards and sound moral and physical conduct;[7] and in 1891, that same court held that a student surrenders a variety of rights upon entering a university.[8] In 1908, a Minnesota court spoke (approvingly) of the doctrine of *in loco parentis* as the rationale that legitimates a college's rules of student conduct;[9] and in 1913, a Kentucky court sustained such rules precisely on grounds of that doctrine.[10]

Item. In 1901, the first community college[11] was established; by 1920 there were 52 such colleges in twenty-three states, and by 1950 more than 300 community colleges, founded and supported by local government, were in operation.[12]

From where, then, comes the current notion that law is a new force with which higher education must reckon? The foregoing illustrations of the historic role of law in academe are unlikely to surprise even the most casual observer of the U.S. scene. Yet knowledgeable people continue to bemoan the awakening of the giant. Two reasons suggest themselves.

First, the commentators who decry recent legal developments in higher education speak pejoratively when using the term intrusion. They do not mean the word to be considered a mere euphemism for the neutral operation of law; it carries instead a negative judgment, the assessment that that operation is disruptive. And by such a standard, the anecdotal evidence above fails as immaterial. Neither *Dartmouth* nor the Morrill Act, for example, is thought by the contemporary critic to have been intrusive, for each strengthened academe (as it is known today). It is not law's operation per se that troubles the critic; it is the jeopardy in which law places cherished values that causes alarm. And who can not distinguish the burden on the institution of the cost of meeting government-reporting requirements from the bounty to the institution of, say, the land-grant legislation?

Second, and similarly, the term law is meant by the critic to be taken more narrowly than it is used in the illustrations above. Law in the comprehensive sense is not the problem, for no one lays claim to a general exception from its reach. Rather, the new and allegedly dangerously intrusive law is that which is born of regulatory intent, is elaborated in regulatory mandate, and is enforced by regulatory process. True, regulation is not the entire concern. The contractual nature of the college catalog; the personal liability of the university administrator; the constitutionality of particular preferential policies; the legal validity of given utilizations of endowment; and so forth all pose nettling difficulties to today's academic practitioner. But the most nettlesome difficulty of all is government regulation of academe.

The regulation by government of various activities in the United

States reaches back at least to 1789 when legislation was enacted authorizing and governing the administration of customs, of ocean vessels, of coastal trade, and of pensions to veterans of the War of Independence. It was not, however, until 1887 that the "administrative agency" was created as such when Congress passed the Interstate Commerce Act, which established the Interstate Commerce Commission. By the 1970s there were hundreds of administrative agencies at the federal and state levels, controlling or monitoring substantial institutionalized activity. Higher education has been a Johnny-come-lately to the scene; but today even higher education is not immune to such oversight, as witness the multitude of coordinating boards now found in more than half the states.

The administrative agency performs quasi-legislative, quasi-judicial, and (though the term is not commonly employed) "quasi-executive" functions. That is, the agency frames and promulgates rules that govern the activities of whatever enterprises fall within its jurisdiction, it adjudicates challenges to and alleged violations of those rules, and, in its "executive" capacity, it investigates and prosecutes such violations.[13] Such an assortment of responsibility and power ostensibly flies in the face of the separation doctrine, which informs most constitutional arrangements in the United States, and demands an explanation of its rationale.

The theory of the regulatory agency rests on the observation that legislatures, which not only enjoy the power but also face the duty of governing a society pervaded by organized esoteric interests, lack the necessary technical competence to fulfill their responsibilities adequately. So they create special bodies expressly designed to serve as their agencies in regulating these complex activities. The delegation, however, of legislative power to the administrative body is not without limit; procedural safeguards must attach to the powers invested in the agency. All parties to be regulated must be afforded: (a) notice of prospective agency action both legislative and judicial;[14] (b) opportunity to be heard; (c) reasonable standards with which to comply; and (d) judicial review of agency action. Moreover, the agency is housed organizationally within the executive branch of government, and is thus affected by personnel and budgetary decisions of the president or governor.

Within the limits of these constraints, the regulatory agency is expected to exercise informed discretion in monitoring and controlling the sector of societal activity that falls to its charge. Neither the Congress and its state counterparts nor the courts will be quick to second-guess substantive determinations brought before them for review, for (again) the presumption underlying the establishment of the agency is that neither courts nor legislatures enjoy the technical competence necessary to the effective regulation of an esoteric activity. What both courts and legislatures do know well, however, are the basic elements of government by law, and each will scrutinize and constrain the agency in its regulatory efforts. The agency's quasi-legislative (that is, rule-making) undertaking, for example, must first meet the procedural requirements of whatever "Administrative Procedure Act" may have been adopted by the Congress or the relevant state legislature for insuring fairness in agency procedures: The federal APA requires that the agency publish advance notice in the *Federal Register* when it is about to establish a proposed substantive rule;[15] that interested parties be afforded opportunity to submit their views on the matter; that the rule as adopted be published no less than thirty days before it is effective; and that interested parties be afforded right of petition for amendment or repeal of the rule.[16] In addition, when a substantive rule thus promulgated is challenged in the courts,[17] it is treated as having all the force of a legislatively enacted statute, thereby triggering all the vulnerabilities of statutes to judicial review of their legal validity. Is the rule in question within the proper jurisdiction of the agency? (That is: Is the agency authorized by its enabling legislation to adopt the rule?) Were the applicable procedural requirements observed in the process of adoption? Does the rule meet all applicable constitutional standards?

The agency's enforcement and adjudicative functions will fare similarly upon review. Deference will be afforded the agency's substantive determinations by legislatures and by courts, here as in rule-making. But both bodies will also define or examine the jurisdictional, procedural, and constitutional validity of the agency's enforcement and quasi-judicial actions.

The reader will find little disagreement among the authors of the following chapters with the theory of government regulation. To the contrary, not only do most acknowledge—some grudgingly, some warmly, some dispassionately—the utility and even occasional necessity of government regulation of higher education, but also none takes issue with the concept of the administrative agency as a regulatory device.[18]

Issues are joined instead at another level. What are the regulatory agencies seeking to accomplish? Is that legitimate? Is it wise? How are they going about their tasks? That is: What are their methods, and what is their competence? What are the probable consequences (intended or not) for academe? What is, what can be, and what should be higher education's response? To set the stage for each chapter, the authors provide a modicum of background material, and, given the relative recency of the development of government regulation in academe, there is some repetition in much of the historical review. Nevertheless, each author approaches the topic with a distinct point of view that enhances or challenges the comments of others.

Fleming, a labor lawyer and university president, finds a major tension in the inevitability of regulation vis-à-vis the enormously complex diversity of U.S. higher education. But he suggests reason for hope in the possibility of scientifically sampled, government-audited, self-regulatory systems in colleges and universities, coupled with incentives to institutions to develop effective dispute-resolution procedures that would diminish the need for government regulation.

Gellhorn and Boyer, students of administrative law and practicing academic administrators, provide a detailed review of the major elements of the regulatory process as applied to academe. In terms not unsympathetic to the rationale of regulation nor to the critical function of higher education in contemporary society, they argue that a right spirit will find opportunity as well as threat in the regulatory process. And in the concluding essay of the collection, Bailey, a student of higher education and one of its most astute thinkers, agrees: Academe's incontrovertible foibles, its demonstrable injustices, its transparent insensitivities at times to the conditions and aspirations of neglected people are matched only by its remarkable capacity to articulate, preserve, transmit, and extend that which is of value in human affairs. The balance must be struck by government between constraints that would cripple higher education's critical social function and a deference that would distill itself ultimately to a grant of unjustified license. But higher education must lead the way.

Fishbein and Ketter clearly disagree. Neither is persuaded that government regulation, especially as it is presently conducted, is either wise or necessary in higher education. Fishbein, general counsel to a major private university, is scandalized both by the manner and substance of regulatory activity to date. To her, the disruptive effects of the procedural requirements alone are disturbing enough, but the suppressive effect of government involvement in the exercise of intellectual judgment has worked inordinate damage to the nation's colleges and universities. Ketter, a civil engineer and president of a major state university, is no less pointed. Cataloging a lengthy series of detriments that he suggests result from government regulation, he sees in accommodation to the regulatory process little hope for change.

Sumberg, watch-dog of government action on behalf of the AAUP, returns the discussion to more conciliatory tones. Addressing the regulatory issue from the perspective of its implications for the academic occupation, he argues that government regulation can and should enhance academe's capacity to further the democratization of society by insuring to the intellectually able an opportunity to play a role in the world of academe. Tobias, however, on grounds of her experience as an affirmative action officer in a private university, submits that government regulation is neither necessary nor sufficient to achieve the results Sumberg endorses, and that in an institution whose administrative leaders are committed to enlarging access to the academic occupation, the task can be accomplished independently of regulatory pressure. On the other hand, Wollett, a student of collective bargaining in education and currently director of a government agency that negotiates labor agreements with unions of state employees, argues that the professoriate has a remarkable capacity to withstand external pressure; he sees little reason to believe that its experience with government regulation will yield contrary results.

Yet the questions remain. Is government regulation of academe actually necessary, not merely inevitable? Or is it at best only helpful (though perhaps still inevitable)? Is it simply "there," both unnecessary and insufficient to the social objectives it pursues? Is it an evil in the academy, destroying much that is precious and offering little in return? Or, when the last argument has been sounded and the last point has been made, will this all have been simply one more storm in higher education's history?

NOTES

1. The remarks that follow lean heavily on E. D. Duryea, "Evolution of University Organization," in J. Perkins, ed., *The University as an Organization* (New York: McGraw-Hill, 1973).

2. "New England's First Fruits, 1643," in R. Hofstadter and W. Smith, eds. American Higher Education: A Documentary History, Vol. I (Chicago: The University of Chicago Press, 1961) p. 6.

3. 4 Wheat. 518.

4. Even such state or public institutions as were maintained followed closely the organizational model of the private colleges. Institutional governance was vested in boards established as public corporations. Duryea, op. cit., p. 20.

5. 8 Barbour 174.

6. D. Potts, " 'College Enthusiasm!' as Public Response, 1800–1860," *Harvard Educational Review* 17 (February 1977): 35–36.

7. 40 Ill. 186.

8. 27 N.E. 54.

9. 104 Minn. 359.

10. 156 Ky. 376.

11. The first private two-year college was established in 1835.

12. G. Parker, *The Enrollment Explosion* (New York: School & Society Books, 1971), p. 94.

13. Not all agencies are empowered by their enabling legislation to perform all the foregoing functions.

14. See note 15 below.

15. Rules may be procedural, interpretative, or substantive. Under the federal APA, only substantive rules face the requirements discussed here. Procedural rules are "housekeeping" rules for internal administration of the agency; though they need not be adopted, the agency must abide by them once it elects to promulgate them. Interpretative rules are prospective, indicating how substantive rules will be applied to various situations. (Adjudications, by contrast, are retrospective, holding for example that a given party has violated a regulation.)

16. The same provision of the act also requires the agency to afford the right of petition for issuance of a rule.

17. Before a court will entertain such a challenge, typically it will require the complainant to exhaust all remedies available within the agency.

18. Which is not to say none would, had they been asked to address that question.

Section I

Government Regulation and Institutional Administration

Chapter 2

Who Will be Regulated, and Why?

Robben W. Fleming

When I was teaching labor law I was impressed with the difficulty of applying a single labor law to the enormously diverse constituencies that made up the American labor movement. The longshoremen on the East and West Coasts were not only in different unions, they had very different traditions. The garment workers were employed in a labor-intensive industry with relatively low capital investments, while the coal miners worked in an industry where capital could readily substitute for labor and thus pose quite different problems. High-productivity industries could offer wages and benefits that restaurants and laundries considered out of the question. The railroads and their unions thought they had model legislation; yet it was an uncomfortable fit for the airlines that were emerging in the transportation field. And the building trade unions often had very different attitudes toward exactly the same problems simply because local traditions were different.

One of the most sensitive problems in government regulation of higher education is the same as the one outlined in the labor law field. Higher education is a vast complex of widely different types of institutions. A measure that applies nicely to one kind of institution has no relevance to another, yet it may be difficult in drafting the regulation to recognize the difference. One can hardly undertake an analysis of the regulation of higher education without pausing at the outset to consider the diversity within the higher education community.

The Carnegie Commission, using 1970 data obtained from the U.S. Office of Education, classified institutions in five categories:[1] (1) doctorate granting; (2) comprehensive universities and colleges; (3) liberal arts colleges; (4) two-year institutions; and (5) specialized institutions. Of the 2,827 institutions they identified, slightly fewer than half (46.4 percent) were public. That figure may be surprising, but the focus here is on institutions, not students. Were one to discuss students, the observation instead would be that almost three-quarters (74.2 percent) attended public institutions. In short, there are more private institutions than public, but the former are smaller than the latter. And differences exist in the powers of government to regulate the private and public sectors.

The specialized schools, as set forth in the Carnegie model, include theological seminaries, medical schools or centers, other health science professional schools, schools of engineering and technology, business and management, art and music, law, teachers colleges, maritime academies, military institutes lacking liberal arts, and so forth. Enrollment in these institutions is shown at more than 280,000. All of the theological seminaries are, of course, private, and the remaining institutions are a mixture of public and private, but a considerable majority of their students are in the private sector.

Numbers, however, do not by any means portray the full panorama of problems that arise when one scratches beneath the surface of the institutions. There are significant differences in the governance structure of institutions and in the expectations of the various academic communities. Faculties, for instance, may expect to participate in the decision-making process in one institution but not in another. Colleges offering religious instruction are private, but they may offer other courses that look exactly like those of any other liberal arts college, and they may wish to qualify for public funds to assist them in their nonreligious efforts. There are women's colleges, men's colleges, Black colleges, and so on. And there are important differences in the social values that prevail in different parts of the country. These factors all pose problems to the legislator who approaches higher education.

The first important point one must make about government regulation of higher education, therefore, is that there is by no means a single academic constituency; higher education is extraordinarily complex, and applicable, effective regulation will be difficult to devise and effect.

THE LEGAL THEORY

It is known to every school child that the Constitution of the United States contemplates a system of government in which there are both delegated and reserved powers. More specifically, the Tenth Amendment to the Constitution reads: "The powers not delegated to the United States by the Constitution, nor prohibited by it to the States, are reserved to the States respectively, or to the people."

Since the Constitution is silent on the issue of education, and the states are not prohibited from maintaining systems of public education, the Tenth Amendment effectively reserves such education to the states. Thus it is that in the United States, unlike most of the other advanced societies of the world, there is no national ministry of education that controls or directs the system of higher education. On the contrary, the operating funds for public universities come primarily from the states and from the tuition that students pay. Public funds that go into private universities raise a different set of problems which will be discussed later.

Despite the clarity of the Tenth Amendment and the well-established historical fact that operating funds for public universities come primarily from the states, it would be inaccurate to conclude that the federal government is without influence in the field of education. Putting aside for the moment questions of legal theory by which such intervention is justified, it may be helpful to remind ourselves how pervasive the federal influence has in fact been.

When President Lincoln signed the Morrill Act in 1862, thereby causing large tracts of public land across the country to be available for sale in support of the establishment of the so-called land-grant institutions, it marked one of the great seminal moments in higher education in America. Not only did the Morrill Act support the founding of a great many of what are now the most prominent public universities in the country, but it started the United States along the path of universally available higher education. It also recognized that agriculture and the industrial arts were a legitimate subject of advanced education; and out of this recognition came a cooperative relationship, financed with federal money, between county agents and schools of agriculture at the great state universities that led in turn to the spectacularly successful increases in agricultural productivity that lead the world to this very day. Also as a consequence of the Morrill Act, Reserve Officer Training Corps (ROTC) programs at universities were instituted, designed to augment the officers corps of the various armed services by offering training at other than military academies. In ensuing wars these programs would surpass the service academies in the number of trained officer personnel they would provide. The presence of such programs on campus would also, in periods of unpopular military adventures, lead to strenuous protests challenging the legitimacy of their campus activities.

Following the momentous events attributable to the Morrill Act, various other kinds of federal activity took place on campus. During World War I, interaction related to the war developed between universities and the government, and in the 1930s many social activities in support of a depressed economy spilled over onto the campuses. For instance, funds were provided for school lunch programs,[2] and many faculty members will remember work programs on college campuses sponsored by the National Youth Administration. Such projects were funded by the federal government, but were directed by the colleges that they supported. Countless students performed tasks comparable to those we would classify today as work-study programs, and that that generation thought of as "on NYA."

With the advent of World War II, the federal role in public and private universities became even more evident. Some campuses, drained of their normal constituency, remained open only because cadres of military trainees were sent there not only to receive some of their military training but also to absorb innumerable sorts of special preparation in enemy languages, cultures, and economies. Those courses were taught by faculty for whom this was their contribution to the war effort. Similarly, the government also recognized that the majority of the nation's scientists were to be found on campuses, and it was to them that the scientific side of military operations turned.

World War II left a legacy of federal government and university interaction, particularly in research. It was evident that military operations would forever after be dominated by scientific expertise of frightening proportions, and that many of these highly sophisticated techniques also had almost unlimited potential for aid to a peaceful world.

Because the best of the research scientists were often in the universities, and because the course of world events had come to depend so heavily on scientific achievement, the National Science Board was created in 1950. It was formed because so many scientists in and out of government recognized that research would be too costly for any but the federal government to support, and because, in the words of its first director, Vannevar Bush "These institutions (the universities, together with the nonprofit research institutes) provide the environment which is most conducive to the creation of new scientific knowledge and least under pressure for immediate, tangible results. . . ."[3]

It was not just science, however, which was to be the focus of federal attention in universities after World War II. There was widespread fear that the American economy could not absorb the millions of GIs who were being released from the military and that the social unrest that would result from high unemployment would be harmful to the country. A brilliant idea for providing education to large numbers of the veterans whose education had been interrupted found expression in the GI Bill, under which veterans were entitled to educational benefits according to their length of service and family status. This resulted in a flood of applicants to universities and in the implementation of extraordinary measures to accommodate them.

Another measure that greatly altered the course of U.S. education was the institution of the Fulbright-Hayes grants, which made use of impounded foreign currencies to support U.S. students and scholars for study abroad. Born out of a new consciousness of this country's role in the world, a new internationalism, and a practical necessity for making constructive use of foreign currencies owed to the United States out of wartime loans, these grants gave higher education a new dimension.

The nature and scope of federal regulation have expanded in the years after World War II, but the basic technique for investing money has remained much the same. The federal government invests dollars in universities for specific purposes and within defined objectives. It supports both mission-oriented and basic research, but within the context of objectives defined by the government. Thus large sums of money have been spent on nuclear projects, space investigation and exploration, the health sciences, and so forth. In the area of student aid, the federal government has helped veterans enjoy an education, partly out of gratitude for their war sacrifices and partly as a hedge against unemployment. It has supported the idea of easy accessibility to higher education by making loans and grants readily available to students, subject to certain stated conditions. It has encouraged certain types of studies such as medicine, dentistry, public health, pharmacy, and nursing by capitation grants that have helped universities expand their facilities. It has made matching grants available for construction when it recognized the need for facilities to accommodate both students and research projects. And it opened the Social Security System to participation by universities, thus helping them provide disability and retirement benefits that might not otherwise be available. (It insisted, however, that the university accept the usual conditions under which such benefits are financed and paid out.)

The common denominator of federal intervention is money—money to help do this if you will do that. All of which brings the discussion back to the question of the basis of the federal government's authority to intervene in an area of national life that is essentially reserved to the states.

Article I, Section 8 of the U.S. Constitution states, "The Congress shall have power to lay and collect taxes [and] provide for the common defense and general welfare of the United States; . . ." Although education is primarily a state function under the Tenth Amendment, nonetheless the federal government can levy and collect taxes for education pursuant to its power to provide for the common defense and general welfare of the United States. In so doing, it can specify how funds, accepted by a university pursuant to a particular federal program, must be spent. Few would argue that the activities that the federal government undertakes in higher education fall outside this umbrella of power. There are, however, some refinements of this doctrine insofar as it pertains to private universities, particularly those that are affiliated with a religious body.

PRIVATE COLLEGES AND UNIVERSITIES

From the legal standpoint, the investment of public funds in public schools as compared with private schools raises somewhat different issues. One must further distinguish between those private schools that are operated by sectarian organizations and those that are not.

As a general proposition, private schools in higher education depend upon three sources of income to support their operations: (1) endowment; (2) annual giving that is sufficiently dependable to be incorporated into the budget; and (3) tuition. In many cases, sectarian institutions substitute income from the parent organization for endowment but otherwise operate on much the same principle. In recent years, private schools have been hard-pressed financially by a combination of circumstances. Inflation has pushed costs up substantially, eroding the value of the dollar. Public university systems have so extended their operations that they are more available geographically and are less costly than private schools. The popular concept of universal access to higher education has pressured all universities, private as well as public, to grant admission without respect to the student's financial capability. Furthermore, some types of research that are expected at any major institution are so costly that they are affordable only if subsidized by public monies. Thus the private universities have had to become more active in their search for public support. And inasmuch as diversity is widely considered a virtue in higher education, legislators have had to take notice of the possibility or even probability that many private colleges and universities will disappear unless they are made eligible for public funds.

The fact that the only Supreme Court case that recognizes the autonomy of colleges and universities from the state legislature is the famous *Dartmouth College* case of 1819 is a good indication of how minimal the legal problems are at the state level in dealing with the problems of private schools, provided they are nonsectarian.[4] States provide tuition differentials for those students who wish to attend private institutions so that both access and diversity can be maintained; facility money is widely available as it is in public institutions; student loans can be secured under state auspices; and at the federal level, student financial aid, research funds, and facility money are available to both public and private institutions. State and federal authorities do, of course, establish conditions for receipt of the available funds and no institution need take the funds if it does not wish to honor the conditions. The power of the purse is, however, a powerful tool, and no matter how true it may be that government funds can be freely declined, in practice few institutions can survive without complying with the conditions that qualify them for public monies. And from a legal point of view, ". . . the fact that a federal [or state] regulation may be annoying, or unfamiliar, or expensive, or even insensitive to academic niceties does not make it unconstitutional."[5]

In short, the serious question is not whether public funds can be given to nonsectarian private education institutions, but rather how far the state can go in imposing conditions on the acceptance of such funds. Some such conditions will flow with the funds regardless of any specific conditions that are attached. By way of example, in the twenty-year period between 1951 and 1971 the National Labor Relations Board changed its view completely as to whether it should assert jurisdiction over union organizations at major private universities. In 1951, the NLRB thought that it would not "effectuate the policies of the Act for the Board to assert its jurisdiction over a nonprofit, educational institution where activities involved are noncommercial in nature and intimately connected with the charitable purposes and educational activities. . . ."[6] By 1971, the board said that it would take jurisdiction over a "private, non-profit" college or university when its operations had a substantial effect on commerce.[7] In reaching the new line of decisions the board considered the large amounts in government appropriations that had allowed the universities to expand their role, the commercial profit realized from housing and food services, the fact that much of the school's income was not from charitable gifts but from income derived from the commercial avenues of securities investments and real estate holdings, and the fact that significant interstate purchases were made. Nor has such reasoning been confined to the area of collective bargaining. Many kinds of social legislation have been and are being applied without successful legal challenge.

Probably the most sensitive of all areas will be the right of colleges and universities to select their own academic personnel. State and federal legislation against discrimination on grounds of sex, age, religion, ethnic origin, and physical handicaps clearly applies to colleges and universities. There are now in the courts a number of cases in which the appointment or promotion procedure is alleged to have produced an adverse decision against an individual who then brought a complaint that the decision was discriminatory. If an outside agency, be it an administrative body or a court, should order the institution to grant tenure or to hire one individual instead of another, the ultimate test will come. Since administrative agencies and courts have for some years ordered employers in business and industry to take such steps, one would have to speculate that they will do likewise in education. Depending upon one's point of view, this may be a very unwise step for the courts to take, but the legality and the wisdom of a particular move are two different issues.

Finally, a word needs to be said about sectarian schools. The First Amendment to the federal Constitution provides that "Congress shall make no law respecting an establishment of religion, or prohibiting the free exercise thereof." That language raises the question whether the federal government can extend financial aid to church-related schools.[8] Over the years the courts have been able to jump that hurdle, replying in the affirmative, and the questions now are to what extent and in what ways such aid may be provided. The current standard was established in a 1971 U.S. Supreme Court case (*Lemon v. Kurtzman*) which offered three criteria for judging the constitutionality of such aid.[9] These were: (1) Does the legislation have a secular purpose? (2) If yes, is the legislation's primary effect to advance or inhibit religion? (3) Does the legislation foster excessive governmental administrative entanglements with religious groups?

By way of illustrating these criteria, it would be too entangling and therefore unconstitutional if the courts found it necessary to police schools to be sure that teachers who received subsidies were not teaching religion. But it would not be unconstitutional to give facility construction money so long as the money was used for secular, neutral, or nonideological services, facilities, or materials.[10] More recent decisions have sought to clarify the rules, particularly in *Roemer v. Board of Public Works of Maryland*.[11] Doubtless refinement of the concept will continue, but the *Roemer* case did suggest that the tests might be more relaxed at the level of higher education than in the kindergarten through twelfth grade system because students were more sophisticated and less likely to be indoctrinated by sectarian views. There are also decisions in which courts have indicated, when deciding on the availability of public funds, that whether or not the student body is all of one religion is significant.[12] This may mean that a sectarian college cannot today deny admission to a student of another faith if the college hopes to be a realistic candidate for public support.

POLICY CONSIDERATION WITH RESPECT TO THE GOVERNMENT'S ROLE

From what has already been said, it is clear that government intervention in the affairs of universities is now pervasive, resting chiefly on the government's power to condition availability of funds on compliance with specific conditions. When one considers the business side of the university, one notes extensive government regulation in the administration of financial aid to students, and of indirect cost allowances in research and other grants; in rules with respect to building construction; in institutional allowances in the form of capitation grants; and so forth.

Social legislation—such as workmen's compensation, unemployment compensation, social security, civil rights, wage and hour laws, collective bargaining laws, occupational safety and health requirements—all of which largely ignored nonprofit institutions in their original enactment, now cover universities. The problem they pose is not one of acceptance of the social objectives that they embody, but of the uncompensated costs they impose on universities in a time of financial stringency.

State laws, and to some extent federal laws, impact on the academic side of the institution in such sensitive areas as admissions and curricula. The state may, and often does, insist on admissibility in state universities of all high school graduates in that state, or on a limitation of out-of-state residents. There is in the courts now the celebrated *Bakke* case from California which will test before the Supreme Court of the United States the legality of special admissions programs for minority students.[13] If the Court holds that universities may not engage in differential practices for such students, it will change the admissions procedures of most universities. And if it rules that universities may continue such practices, that may encourage Congress to set aside special funds for the educational advancement of minority groups, a possibility which is now thought doubtful.

In the matter of curriculum, the powers of both state and federal governments are also evident. State boards of education or legislatures regularly assert their power to deny funding to a curriculum which is deemed unneeded or duplicative. The federal government through its funding incentives encouraged development of the aerospace programs in a period of national interest in that subject, and is now repeating the process in a medical area, family practice, because the specialty is thought to represent a neglected field of study.

In the area of employment of personnel, civil rights legislation at both the state and federal level requires that there be no discrimination in hiring and that affirmative action be taken to rectify past wrongs. No more sensitive probe could be made into the life of the university than to intervene in the appointment of faculty members, yet it is being done.

The accreditation of institutions of higher education is usually undertaken by private associations. But both state and federal governments have asserted their authority to assume this function, and one must believe that, at a minimum, they could use their funding power if they wish to accomplish this objective.

Even the size of classes in state universities is largely a function of the level of public funding, and the same is true of private universities insofar as they look to either the state or federal government for a critical portion of their total budget. In *Rackin v. University of Pennsylvania*,[14] the court noted that while only 7 to 11 percent of the university's current operating income came from the state, that proportion was nonetheless of critical importance in maintaining the quality of the basic educational enterprise.

Given the long history of governmental support of education, and the eagerness with which higher educational institutions have sought public money, one asks why, at this moment in time, there is all the furor over government intervention. But little reflection is necessary to find the major threads in the current disenchantment.

Finance

Almost all of higher education, whether public or private, is in a cost squeeze, and the situation is likely to get worse before it gets better. Federal funds which support so many projects within universities have been steadily decreasing, particularly given the devaluation of the dollar. Faced with high unemployment and welfare costs, states also have tightened their belts, and higher education has taken more than its share of the cutbacks.

In the midst of an already troubled effort to attain financial stability, universities see themselves as the victims of capricious federal funding action that at one time encourages them to expand certain programs and then suddenly withdraws the funding, as in the case of the capitation grants for the health sciences. Simultaneously, state and federal legislative bodies take the entirely laudable step of covering employees of nonprofit institutions by such protective legislation as unemployment and workmen's compensation without, at the same time, providing the institutions with sufficient funds to pay the resulting bills.

To make matters worse, university personnel find themselves spending an inordinate amount of time completing endless forms and reports, many of which are known to go unread because there is no one at the other end with time enough to read them. The reporting requirement, moreover, imposes additional administrative costs on the university and additional burdens on the faculty (who can hardly be said to be working at their highest skill in the completion of forms).

Civil Rights

Apart from their financial effects, some of the new regulations are highly divisive. The best example, of course, is civil rights legislation. Our nation's past is too apparent for anyone seriously to deny that discrimination has taken place. Thus, women and minorities whose experience suggests that they have not been given equal access to the general labor market find it hard to believe that the traditional faculty hiring system will treat them fairly. At the same time, faculties who picture themselves as always seeking to hire the most qualified person available view any suggestion of a "goal" or "quota" in women or minority appointments as a move that, if pursued mechanistically, will destroy the academic quality of the institution. Since there is no national consensus as to the rules of the new game, the enforcement machinery flounders while both government and university administrators ponder how to resolve the dilemma. And the unrest that grows as a result of the delay contributes heavily to the sense of insecurity and tension between government bodies and the educational institutions.

Social Security

Time and circumstances change the way any given issue is regarded. Prior to 1950, when university personnel were not covered by the Social Security Act, there was considerable agitation to obtain coverage because so many were without disability or pension coverage. When Congress finally passed a bill embracing employees in nonprofit concerns, there was joy in academia. But today academic associations consider withdrawing from participation in the Social Security program. The reason is simple. Both the taxable base and the tax rate for Social Security purposes rise inexorably. To the astonishment of some students of the system, individuals have not protested vigorously. But universities, caught in a larger financial crisis, find that Social Security payments constitute an enormously large expenditure for which their resources are inadequate. Under the circumstances, it is not surprising that they are frustrated.

Independence

There is among academics a special sensitivity to the independence of the university, and to the fact that government can at almost any moment completely overwhelm the institution. They are frightened by the fact that in many other countries the university is the complete handservant of the government. They share a deeply held conviction that the university must be free, however awkward this may be, or however annoying to the government, because without that freedom the nation will ultimately suffer.

So there is grumbling today between the government and the universities, often framed as legal questions to be decided in the courts. The *Bakke* case, for example, may tell us a good deal about the future of minority education, and certainly there will be further probes as to how far the states can go in assisting sectarian schools. Nevertheless, in the last analysis it is hard to cast the question, "How much regulation, and why?" as a judicial issue. The power of both state and federal governments to induce desired conduct by offering funds on condition of compliance appears to be overpowering, at least if the governments show constraint in areas that might otherwise run afoul of the First or Tenth Amendments to the U.S. Constitution. If the present uneasiness is to be quieted, it must be because an accommodation is reached between the power and wisdom of governmental intervention in universities.

CONCLUSIONS

Despite dissatisfaction with current government controls over higher education, such controls are unlikely to decrease. Indeed, the odds are that they will increase. This is because: (1) enormous amounts of money are involved and the public will insist upon an accounting; (2) political pressures to apply social legislation to universities will be sustained at a high level; and (3) as a people we still manifest an almost knee-jerk reaction to problems by enacting laws expected to solve them. Thus we see more and more pressure at the state level to coordinate higher education in order to eliminate duplication. The terms are ill-defined and the results in states that have already made the effort are unimpressive. Yet the momentum continues. At the federal level both the president and the secretary of Health, Education and Welfare are on record as wishing to simplify paperwork and controls. Yet the secretary has already said that abuses of financial aid at the college level constitute a great problem and that he expects to move against such abuses quickly. The history of administrative controls suggests that it is easier to add new measures than to abolish old ones.

There is little optimism that the amount of either state or federal regulation will decrease. There is, however, some basis for hope that it will, over a period of time, be better administered. There is agreement on the nature of many of the defects in the present system, and the personal relationships between university and government people are cordial, if uneasy. The root of the difficulty is in the complexity of the administrative problem. Both government and university personnel are conscious of the degree to which overlapping jurisdictions on a single problem complicates the lives of those who must enforce regulations and of those who are the object of the regulations.

There are, however, signs of hope. Toward the end of the Ford Administration a task force worked hard to reduce the paperwork requirements that preoccupy university personnel. Some constructive recommendations were made. There is evidence that the Office of Management and Budget is taking these and other similar recommendations seriously, and that the president himself has urged simplification of required reports. Perhaps we will see movement on that front.

The greatest hope for improvement in government regulation of higher education lies in a system that combines scientific sampling of self-regulatory systems with an incentive for developing private grievance procedures that will finally resolve the bulk of the disputes. While this approach will be opposed by many critics as less than ideal, and it is, the proper question is not whether such a plan would be perfect, but whether it would be better than anything we have tried so far.

What I have said earlier indicates that the Constitution and the efforts of state and federal legislative bodies to regulate higher education indicate that our legal forms will tolerate most of the kinds of government regulation that are likely to be attempted. The major question, therefore, is not whether such regulation is legal, but whether there is wisdom in trying to resolve all of our problems by government action.

NOTES

1. Carnegie Commission on Higher Education, A Classification of Institutions of Higher Education 1–7 (1973).

2. A. Lapati, Education and the Federal Government (1975).

3. V. Bush, Science the Endless Frontier (1945).

4. 4 Wheat. 518.

5. O'Neil, *God and Government at Yale: The Limits of Federal Regulation of Higher Education,* 44 U. Cin. L. Rev. 525 (1975).

6. 97 N.L.R.B. 424, 427.

7. 183 N.L.R.B. 329.

8. *See* Note, *Private Colleges, State Aid, and the Establishment Clause,* 1975 Duke L.J. 976; Mott & Edelstein, *Church, State, and Education: The Supreme Court and its Critics,* 2 J. Law & Educ. 535 (1973).

9. 503 U.S. 602.

10. *Id.* at 625.

11. 96 S. Ct. 2337.

12. In Tilton v. Richardson (403 U.S. 672, 686), the Court noted that

non-Catholics were admitted as students and given faculty appointments. In Hunt v. McNair (413 U.S. 734, 743–44), the Court found that the Baptist College at Charleston was "oriented significantly towards secular rather than sectarian education," despite its close ties with the South Carolina Baptist Convention. It was important that:

> What little there is in the record concerning the College establishes that there are no religious qualifications for faculty membership or student admission, and that only 60% of the college student body is Baptist, a percentage roughly equivalent to the percentage of Baptists in that area of South Carolina.

One of the district court findings considered by the Court in Roemer v. Board of Public Works of Maryland (96 S. Ct. at 2350), was that "the student bodies are chosen without regard to religion."

13. 18 Cal. 3d 34, 553 P.2d 1152, 132 Cal. Rptr. 680, *cert. granted*, 97 S. Ct. 1098 (No. 76–811).

14. 386 F. Supp. 992.

Chapter 3

The Academy As A Regulated Industry

Ernest Gellhorn
Barry B. Boyer

INTRODUCTION

In 1975 the presidents of the nation's two most prestigious universities, Harvard and Yale, challenged the federal government's role in higher education. Addressing a distinguished group of lawyers, then President Kingman Brewster of Yale thundered: "High on the agenda of the [legal] profession, especially its scholarly branch, should be to see that in both limits on authority and redress against its abuse, the coercive power of the federal purse [over higher education] is made subject to the rule of law."[1] Harvard President Bok's attack included no less strident a warning. He cautioned Harvard's powerful alumni that "the critical issue for the next generation is Harvard's independence and freedom from governmental restraint."[2]

What has come of this double-barrelled attack on what Brewster called "clumsy bureaucratic interference" in the administration of higher education? Have there been major changes in the practices of the government regulators, or have doubts been raised about the theoretical underpinnings of government regulation comparable to those being directed at economic regulation of private business? No authoritative answers to these questions are possible since the streams of new regulations and regulatory programs—and the critiques by educators—continue to flow unabated while reliable empirical data are scarce. Nevertheless, the issues raised by the critics of government regulation of higher education are sufficiently serious to justify close scrutiny and evaluation, even if the conclusions remain tentative.

One such evaluation has already focused on the constitutional basis of Brewster's challenge. In 1975, Robert O'Neill, now vice president of the Bloomington campus of the University of Indiana, examined the four areas where the concern about unconstitutional encroachment by federal regulation might be tested.[3] But in each case, after the charges had been examined carefully and the supportive evidence sifted and evaluated, he determined that the constitutional challenge was unfounded. In each area the government's authority to regulate higher education could be easily sustained. That is, (1) the restrictions imposed by HEW and other government agencies were not unrelated to the legitimate objectives of the programs and activities they supported; (2) the conditions attached to federal funding did not indirectly seek results that the federal government was barred from achieving directly; (3) the federal regulations did not compel institutions of higher education to violate anyone's constitutional rights; (4) and the restrictions imposed by federal regulation did not threaten the educational autonomy of universities and colleges. Thus O'Neill concluded that "Brewster overstates the case when he implies that current regulation reaches or exceeds those limits."[4]

In this chapter, we consider another volley in the Bok-Brewster broadside, namely, the "stifling bureaucratic requirements" that President Bok complained impose mounting costs on universities without corresponding benefits to either students or the public. Our concern is not whether government regulation is effective in achieving its stated goals, nor whether particular regulatory programs affecting higher education embody sound public policies. Our interest here is more narrowly drawn: are the procedural constraints that arise from increasing federal regulation of higher education as unreasonable and destructive as their distinguished critics have claimed?

This confined field of inquiry contains difficult issues of fundamental importance. Procedures are the contact points at which the broad social policies embodied in regulatory statutes take on operational reality in the daily life of the institution. Thus, to a large degree, the quality of the administrative process can determine the effect that regulatory programs will have in practice. Moreover, the critics have not limited their attacks to the details of the regulatory process, such as the draftsmanship of rules or the quality of administration. Rather, their challenge goes deeper—it is targeted at the theory, purpose, and legitimacy of government intervention in higher education—and must be assessed on that basis.[5]

This point is important because mistakes have been made in implementing the recent regulatory programs, and more will undoubtedly occur. Indeed, it may well be true that there is a disturbingly high degree of inadequate, inefficient, and ineffective regulation in the programs affecting higher education. But that alone would not necessarily make the case against such regulations since these costs must be weighed against the benefits that can be realized from the regulatory programs and the probability that conditions will improve. The recent wave of regulatory activities affecting universities is forcing major changes in established modes of conduct, and change inevitably introduces stress—especially change that comes from attempts to regulate a moving, growing force like higher education.

In assessing the current problems that colleges and universities have in coping with increased government regulation, it should be remembered that higher education has shown flexibility and resourcefulness in adapting to shifting social realities over the past thirty years. The reasons underlying these changes, moreover, tell us something about the contemporary regulatory response. Perhaps the first major event was the return of veterans after the Second World War and the Korean conflict, which swelled the enrollments of our universities, introduced government support of student tuition, and undermined the justification for parietal rules. Another was the wave of political attacks on professorial loyalty during the 1950s. The universities claimed unfairness and lack of due process, and in time these principles of procedural justice came back to govern (sometimes to haunt) aspects of universities' relationships with their students, faculty, and employees. This was followed by the massive infusion of federal aid to education in the post-Sputnik era, the civil rights and women's movements, and finally the Vietnam War protests, all of which have altered not only the prevailing practices and standards but also the attitudes and expectations of those who are involved in higher education.

These are only a few of the many events that have transformed higher education. But they are enough to illustrate our initial point— that the universities no longer stand apart (if they ever did) from the main currents of society. Indeed, the universities have often been a major motivating force for social change, supplying both the intellectual blueprint for government action and the personnel to implement it. The "Brain Trust" of the Roosevelt Administration, the "Best and the Brightest" of the Kennedy era, the civil rights and antipoverty programs, and the movement to end the war in Vietnam all drew heavily on academic support.

Beyond its direct involvement in the formation and implementation of public policy, the contemporary university wields several other kinds of social power. A large university can dominate the economic life of the surrounding community in its roles as a major consumer of goods and services, and as an employer. In the aggregate, institutions of higher learning comprise a significant sector of the national economy. Moreover, they increasingly control the individual's access to economic goods. In a specialized technological society, the universities assume the role of gatekeepers controlling access to employment opportunities, and thus to wealth, power, and influence. It is hardly surprising, therefore, that some segments of society would think it desirable, if not essential, to assure that higher education be accountable and responsive to public needs.[6]

The theoretical and practical underpinnings of government regulation of higher education, we believe, are firmly established and likely to endure. Universities are too important a force in society to escape the contemporary demands for fairness, openness, equality of opportunity, and accountability that are being pressed upon all large and powerful institutions. And the processes and techniques of administrative regulation, imperfect as they are, may well be the most practicable means of achieving these goals.

If the goals of regulation seem worthy, why then have educators so frequently reacted with hostility and alarm to the imposition of new regulatory requirements? A large part of the opposition seems to arise from the inevitable friction created when substantial, rapid changes are imposed on large organizations. Change is especially disquieting when it is implemented by a bureaucracy unfamiliar with the special needs, values, and problems of higher education. Moreover, the kinds of procedural changes with which we are concerned—open decision-making, widespread participatory rights, more reasoned and explained decisions, and the development of ongoing relationships with external regulators—alter distributions of power within the university. They also modify perceptions and change expectations. It should not be surprising, therefore, that university leaders and constituencies may sense a real threat to the security of their positions.

Another major factor in academia's resistance to government regulation is what President Robben Fleming of the University of Michigan has identified as the "cost squeeze."[7] Complying with regulatory requirements can impose major expenses on the universities, and the current wave of federal regulation has come at a time when most institutions of higher learning are facing austere budgets, declining enrollments, and sharply rising costs. At the same time, the social benefits sought through some regulatory programs may seem trivial or nonexistent by the time the program goals have been translated from the broad generalities of statutory policy to the operational realities of administrative regulations. Few academics, for example, would argue that sex discrimination in higher education should not be eliminated. Yet many have questioned the wisdom of pushing this general principle to the particular conclusion that expenditures on intercollegiate athletics should be absolutely equalized between the sexes.

Finally, some part of the resistance to government regulation may be directed at the less tangible, more symbolic aspects of the regulatory process. The fact that the political institutions of society have felt it necessary to impose a system of regulation on the universities implies a judgment that higher education, like business or the professions, cannot be trusted to serve the public interest on its own initiative. Where trust in a university's accounting procedures was the rule of the past, accountability is the current watchword. Given the extraordinary record of abuses of public trust by powerful institutions inside and outside of government during the past decade, it is understandable that the public is skeptical and suspicious. In any event, the large amounts of public money flowing into higher education probably would have brought a demand for greater controls on the use of those funds. Still, the academic community reacts with surprise and resentment to this questioning of its integrity. Many academicians are also quite sensitive—perhaps more so than the general public—to the symbolic aspects of bureaucracy, the image of red tape, interminable delays, rigid rules, and stultifying uniformity. In part, this response may reflect a general temperamental characteristic of those who have chosen the academic life; in part, it may arise from the belief that bureaucracy tends to respond only to gross, quantifiable, demonstrably utilitarian "inputs and outputs," and therefore may be indifferent or hostile to important academic values.

In some respects the concerns are well founded; but despite these kinds of problems, we believe that the overall picture of the emerging regulatory environment is by no means as bleak as the critics have described. Higher education is still in the early stages of adjustment to broad federal regulation, and first tries seldom reach perfect accommodations. The administrative process provides a variety of tools that can be used to affect the nature, scope, and direction of necessary adjustments. If the leadership of higher education continues to develop the understanding and the skill to use these tools effectively, many of the rough edges of the regulatory process can be smoothed.

There are also positive benefits that can flow from higher education's involvement in the regulatory process, beyond the crucial financial support that government provides. Regulatory programs are designed to implement policies of broad importance to the society such as equality of opportunity, fairness to workers and students, and occupational safety, which ought to guide the actions of the universities. When regulatory procedures are well-designed and properly used, they can make it possible to achieve these policy goals. By increasing the accountability of the universities, administrative procedures also can help higher education maintain the confidence of its constituencies and of the general public. More importantly, the procedures and techniques of the regulatory process can improve the way major decisions are made and implemented within the universities. The underlying values of administrative procedures are openness, rationality, fairness, efficiency, and accountability. And these, we believe, are not inconsistent with the goals of the university.

THE CONTROL OF DISCRETION INSIDE THE UNIVERSITY

Only in recent years have suggestions been made to limit administration discretion. Before then the general rule was that university administrations were seldom questioned in the governance of their institutions.[8] Trustees and regents quietly affirmed policy choices; their offices were positions of honor and prestige, not power bases for policy-making. University presidents and provosts declared policy; consultations with those affected were usually held only after basic decisions had been made and sometimes even implemented. Appointment, promotion, and tenure of faculties (as well as of other university employees) were matters of grace determined by departmental chairmen and college deans with little guidance from, much less interference by, other faculty members or the affected individuals. Curricular decisions were made by faculties, it is true, but without serious student input and with little change over time. Admissions decisions went almost by default since there were few pressures to change old enrollment patterns. Student conduct was subject to rules drafted by universities in their roles as surrogate parents, and while their subjects did not always applaud the rules, they did not seriously challenge them or their application. To paraphrase Justice Holmes, no one had a right to a university education or to be a teacher, and therefore university students and teachers had no rights. If dissatisfied with the rules or their application, one could choose another institution or field; no forum was available to raise questions or to obtain redress. A university education, whether from a public or private institution, was a matter of privilege, and therefore its grant or denial could not be questioned.

Even this summary description of educational administration in previous years is testimony to the scope and speed of the changes that have occurred in higher education. Changing enrollment patterns, rising costs, widespread inflation, diminishing incomes, and austere state budgets have all contributed to much closer policy oversight. Similarly, as the campuses have become more involved in public policy, the makers of that policy have become interested in what is going on there. But the most significant changes have been in the expanding role of students and faculty and the narrowing of discretion allowed educational administrators. These changes are reflected in the arguments and rules made by courts in setting the outer limits on the authority and discretion of these participants.

Perhaps the most basic and far-reaching change that has occurred within higher education is the set of limitations now placed on educator choice by requiring that decision standards be spelled out and that fair procedures for applying standards be developed.[9] Requirements of this nature are important to students and teachers, and to educational institutions, as well as to the public interest. These new controls on higher education are outlined here because the requirements and their rationales are often not considered and because they are typical of the broader picture. In most instances they have been initiated by courts rather than by the executive (HEW) or legislative (Congress) branches of government. As such they reflect broader changes in society and changing attitudes toward authority.

Judicial Controls[10]

An early and basic change in the discretion allowed university administrators was due not to federal funding or executive interference through regulations and procedures but to judicial reactions to findings that educational institutions had overstepped reasonable bounds in regulating student conduct. Courts had been and still are reluctant to intervene. If it is established, however, that administrative discretion has been abused and important interests have not been adequately protected, then discretion will be limited and new procedures required.

In the process of making this change from no supervision to a limited oversight, a new set of standards and theories has emerged. These are reflected in the arguments now being accepted concerning the universities' role with regard to student conduct. Courts once deferred to educator decisions because (1) the universities and their administrators were acting *in loco parentis* to their students; (2) educators rather than judges were in the best position to determine the students' general welfare; (3) education was a privilege to which universities could attach almost any condition; (4) the schools had reserved full powers in their admission contracts with students; (5) academic independence should be preserved and educational expertise recognized, which meant that decisions by educators should not be second-guessed by courts; (6) and the schools had been granted plenary authority by their state legislators. The failure of these arguments to uphold educator decisions is almost total. The demise of the right-privilege distinction, prevalent in the law governing administrative agencies, is now also reflected in decisions dealing with educational administration, although some distinctions allowing special status for the university are retained.

The Supreme Court's decision in *Healy v. James*,[11] is illustrative and instructive. It involved a state college's refusal to recognize (or permit use of its facilities to) a local chapter of the Students for a Democratic Society (SDS). On review by the Supreme Court, it was held that the student's first amendment rights of association barred the college from refusing recognition to the SDS chapter because of the chapter's unconventional views. The students' success was not total, however. In recognizing student rights and limiting the college's discretion, the Court also noted that the educational environment allowed campus officials greater control of speech and related rights on campus than off. Thus the Court was not in fact overturning educator discretion; rather, it was carefully defining and confining it within specific boundaries. Within a university the traditional first amendment standard requiring a clear and present danger before speech could be inhibited was altered. The test became one of material and substantial disruption of campus activities. And it therefore followed that the college could deny recognition to an organization only if it refused to obey reasonable rules for maintaining order.

The *Healy* decision is significant for several reasons. It is a product of the conservative Burger Court, not the Warren court of the 1960s. It establishes, along with other cases, that constitutional rights do apply in the educational context; yet those rights may be restricted in narrow circumstances if justified by the educational environment. It is interesting to note that the Court in *Healy* viewed itself—and we think rightly—as the protector of academic and political freedom from encroachment by the university. In this role, the Court was unwilling to accept the educators' uncontrolled judgment of what was required on the campus because other important interests were at stake.

It is also important to note that this recognition of judicially protected interests reflected more than mere disenchantment with past decisions by educational administrators—undoubtedly a factor in many decisions limiting educator discretion—for the Court clearly was seeking to protect interests previously slighted. It therefore reflects changing societal conditions as well as attitudes. Education, in other words, is no longer a luxury for the few but a necessity for all; and those qualified for higher education are entitled to take advantage of its opportunities for employment, enrichment, and position. Because higher education has increasingly been subsidized by taxpayer dollars, it has become a property right available to all. In addition, student independence and maturity, generally recognized at an earlier age (for example, the eighteen-year-old vote), undercut parietal rules as the schools continued to impose conditions parents had previously abandoned.

Schools make a variety of judgments, some procedural and others substantive, some disciplinary and others academic. Still others involve employment and resource allocations. The extent to which courts insert their judgment and protect interests adversely affected by school decisions depends largely on the judgment involved and the interest affected. Thus, as illustrated in *Healy*, although the educational environment may modify the application of constitutional guarantees, an educational institution's substantive judgments may not infringe upon a student's (or a teacher's) constitutional rights of speech, press, or association.[12] Substantive codes of student conduct have also been regulated where vague and unclear. Codes that merely prohibit "misconduct," for example, will not stand if a person of ordinary intelligence does not know what is required. Educators have attacked these decisions on the grounds that they impose legalistic models that impair the educational environment, a prediction that has not come true. While colleges and universities do not have to draft rules with the specificity of a criminal code, the university's flexibility is no greater than that generally accorded public employers or governments when allocating public benefits.[13]

However, courts have been quite willing to oversee the process by which students are disciplined. In the landmark case of *Dixon v. Alabama State Board of Education*,[14] a lower court held that notice and a hearing were prerequisites to the expulsion of college students for misconduct. That is, students must be given a statement of the specific charges and the grounds that justify expulsion as well as the names of opposing witnesses, a report of the facts to which the witnesses testified, a full opportunity to present their own defense, and access to the findings and conclusions of the governing board. Despite these requirements, a complete trial-type hearing with lawyers present, subpoena powers, and so forth, generally has not been required. And in approving a less stringent procedure for suspending high school students, the Supreme Court has made clear its basic agreement with the *Dixon* ruling.[15] In recognizing basic notions of fairness and fair process, the courts are also aware that trial-type procedures are not the only alternative. Management tools or negotiating processes that reflect concerns for accuracy and integrity in the decision-making process, for example, may be acceptable alternatives.

Underlying many of these cases is a sense that where the judgments being made are conventional, legal determinations that courts are accustomed to making and on which educators have no special competence, judicial examination of university processes can be close and exacting. However, judicial concern for educator control of the educational environment has affected their choice of required safeguards. Moreover, only where basic constitutional rights are implicated have courts gone beyond reviewing methods and substituted their judgments for the educator's.

This active judicial role in the discipline arena has not been transferred to the review either of academic judgments or of administrative decisions regarding a school's institutional objectives or its allocation of resources. In the case of academic judgments, the courts have demonstrated significant reluctance even to enter the arena. Little more is required of institutions as a substantive standard than that the decision not be arbitrary or capricious, and that the burden of proof (which, as every teacher knows, is practically insurmountable) be on the student. The reasons seem obvious. Given the volume of academic judgments made by every institution of higher education, their work could all but stop if procedural guarantees such as notice and hearing were imposed every time a student was unhappy with a grade. Individual academic judgments have long been considered part of the faculty's academic freedom. And it seems virtually impossible to construct procedural reforms that would not occasion second-guessing and gross invasion of the teacher's prerogatives. The resulting deference given academic questions, even on procedural grounds, is unique.[16]

When it comes to reviewing resource allocation decisions, even this limited oversight has been foregone. The Supreme Court has declared such questions essentially beyond judicial control.[17]

Administrative Controls

The announcement and occasional enforcement of judicial controls is only the first step. As the aftermath of *Brown v. Board of Education* illustrates, where important social changes are at stake other events may have to occur for court orders to have an impact. While perhaps not of the same magnitude, the due process revolution in higher education did not happen overnight. Thus, the more important occurrence has been the establishment during the past decade of internal controls by governing boards and administrators on the discretion exercised throughout higher education. The adoption of procedures designed to assure a fair process has forced numerous changes, but they have been concentrated in two areas. First, most universities have careful procedures governing student expulsions for misconduct (as well as other areas) that guarantee the affected student a "fair hearing" before an adverse decision is made. Second, these institutions have also established codes or adopted standards that are applied in these hearings. Without such standards the results could be arbitrary and unreasonable; but with these guides, if applied in a fair process, the results should be uniform and rational.

Most institutions have followed sound legal advice and intelligent policy by being intentionally overinclusive in their rules. They have adopted additional procedures and standards, even where unrestrained administrative discretion might be upheld. Thus, the scope of these additions to the processes of higher education has not been limited to case law requirements. Moreover, and perhaps as a result of these efforts, there has been a change in attitudes and mores. What was once considered absolutely necessary administrative authority in the interest of educational autonomy and administrative efficiency is now acknowledged to be unnecessary. The advantages of shared authority, with the possibility of greater responsiveness from and responsibility by students and faculty, have resulted in substantial extensions of once radical ideas. The universities have rediscovered an age-old truth of law: The development of fair procedures need not impair efficiency and may in fact contribute to the integrity of institutional decision-making.

The elements of fair procedure, as they have been worked out in the courts and through experience in the universities and colleges where facts are in dispute, are now well established. Four basic features are commonly included:

1. *Notice* of the charges must be given to the person to be charged. Knowing the charges is the first step in preparing to meet them, and energy and resources will not be spent (by either side) on matters not being charged. A notice requirement also establishes charges the university must sustain.
2. A *hearing* must be held for the charged person to hear and challenge the evidence presented as well as to present affirmative evidence in his or her own behalf. Evidence not presented in the hearing cannot be relied upon since it defeats the essence of a fair hearing (the opportunity to challenge and rebut opposing evidence). Hearing procedures must be designed to assure that the tribunal will have before it all the evidence it needs to decide the matter.
3. A *neutral tribunal* that decides the matter, based upon the evidence presented, is also essential to a fair hearing. The absence of bias and the independence of the tribunal are prerequisites if the hearing officer's decision is to be acceptable to the person charged.
4. A *reasoned decision* is a recent addition in many circumstances.

This element usually includes stating the findings and giving reasons to support the conclusion reached. It assures that the institution's articulated standards have been applied uniformly and it provides visible evidence of the integrity of the decisional process.

5. Though not required, in practice educational institutions have added a fifth feature as a further safety check, namely, the *opportunity for review* by a superior official of an adverse decision. No process can assure complete accuracy or avoid all mistakes, and it is not uncommon for those on a lower rung of authority to impose relatively harsh remedies. Therefore, while superior officers seldom reverse unfavorable decisions, they frequently adjust the penalties downward.

These or similar procedures, then, are followed today in student (and employee) disciplinary proceedings where fact issues predominate. Similar but less formalized procedures often govern questions of residence which determine whether in-state–out-state quotas and tuition apply. But most questions involving discretion—such as student admissions, faculty hiring, and promotion—where such procedures might seem applicable also involve subjective judgment. Here administrative discretion seems particularly important. Thus, while some concessions to "trial-type" procedures have been made, compromises have been required. Still, the change from the very recent past is startling.

Consider, for example, faculty promotion and tenure. Less than a decade ago, not a long time in institutional terms, the procedure for promotion and tenure was rudimentary. No one mentioned the matter to the candidate in advance, no resume or list of writings was sought, no interview was conducted. Indeed, the candidate was often completely unaware that the faculty was even considering the question. And the faculty apparently reached its decision without a committee report, close consideration of teaching performance, or even a reading of the candidate's scholarship.

Now compare the process as it is developing today. Each year every probationary candidate's activities are evaluated by a college committee and summarized for the dean; individual discussions are held with the candidate to review his or her progress. Specific standards must be met that have been adopted by the university as the measures of performance. At the time the primary decision is to be made, the candidate usually prepares a memorandum outlining his or her teaching responsibilities, writing and other scholarly activities, university and community service, and so forth. The committee then reviews the writings, attends classes, often interviews students, sometimes communicates with scholars in the candidate's field, reads student evaluations, and considers other evidence. The candidate may submit evidence and even seek an interview. An open hearing is not held, however, because of the need for candor and the necessity for maintaining an ongoing relationship with the candidate. Participation by close colleagues in the process is apparently viewed as an adequate substitute. The committee then submits its recommendations to the faculty. If an adverse recommendation is made, the candidate may be given an opportunity to respond. Usually, however, a supporting colleague makes the case. The faculty is also provided with a copy of the candidate's resume and urged to read his or her writings. The matter is then considered de novo. And this process continues on to a separate review by the dean and a university-wide committee with an opportunity in some instances to respond to an adverse recommendation along the way.

Additional details might also be mentioned, but enough has been said to make the point. Current procedures obviously seem much fairer to the candidate. They also provide greater assurance to the university that an accurate yet rigorous judgment has been made. There is no question that much more faculty and administrative time and effort are consumed. But this is not necessarily at greater cost to the university. In fact, these added procedures and reliance on articulated standards do not necessarily mean that more candidates are given tenure and promoted or that standards have been lowered. Indeed, the opposite has occurred if one examines the numbers or compares the scholarship of today's tenure denials (and approvals) with those of a decade ago. Without placing too much emphasis on these numbers or subjective arguments, inasmuch as other factors may also be at play, we simply note that procedural and substantive due processes are not necessarily at war with the interests of higher educational institutions.

A review of admissions decisions, especially of the professional schools facing enrollment pressures, reveals a less formalized procedure but a similar and significant change in process. Other areas of discretion, such as student placement and references, grades and academic honors, and teaching loads and salaries to name a few, usually have not been affected, at least in the absence of faculty unions. But it does seem that further changes, similar to those that occurred in faculty promotion and tenure, will occur in areas such as those just mentioned. That is to say, deans and department chairmen are now checking with faculty on teaching assignments and loads before they make their decisions. And decisions on leaves and sabbaticals are no longer matters left solely to administrative grace. On the other hand, additional concerns are still considered in determining whether to limit the scope and significance of any changes. Self-interest, for example, is likely to skew faculty judgments on salaries and layoffs; and if excellence is to be a university's standard, faculty input will continue to be limited in this area. Similar reasons will preclude student participation in the determination of grades and academic honors.

In other words, there is a range of procedures and standards in use by institutions of higher education for limiting the discretion of administrators. As the fact component of decisions to be made increases, it is likely that trial-type requirements will be relied upon. And as non-quantifiable judgments are involved, less formalized processes will be used. Nevertheless, basic notions of notice and opportunity to be heard are already common in either case and are likely to occupy an ever larger portion of every university's procedural terrain.

OPENNESS, CONFIDENTIALITY, AND CONTROLS OVER INFORMATION

Paralleling the rapid evolution of "administrative due process" has been the even more rapid emergence of laws designed to govern the use and control of sensitive information. At the federal level alone, legislation has forced numerous major changes in information-management practices over the past dozen years. Broad disclosure of government files became the rule through the enactment[18] and amendment[19] of the Freedom of Information Act; regulatory agency meetings have been opened to the public under the Government-in-the-Sunshine[20] and Federal Advisory Committee Acts;[21] protections against governmental abuse of sensitive personal information were provided by the Privacy Act of 1974;[22] and minimum standards for use of consumer credit information were established by the Fair Credit Reporting Act,[23] the Fair Credit Billing Act,[24] and the Equal Credit Opportunity Act.[25] The state legislatures have also been active, and most states have either enacted or amended "open government" statutes during this period. More inclusive and more detailed information-control laws may be forthcoming, if one can judge from the sweeping legislative agenda that was recently recommended by the federal Privacy Protection Study Commission.[26]

This outpouring of legislation reflects a broad-based social demand to hold accountable the large bureaucracies in both the public and private sectors. Recent history provides numerous illustrations of the proposition that power flowing from the creation, collection, analysis, transfer, and disclosure of information can easily be abused. While the requirements of administrative due process described above provide some protection against arbitrariness when this power is exercised in relatively formal decisions, the information-control statutes generally seek to extend and adopt the procedural safeguards to a wide array of less formal, less visible, but no less important forms of bureaucratic decision-making.

These underlying concerns are evident in the federal information law that is of most direct concern to higher education: the Family Educational Rights and Privacy Act,[27] officially known by the acronym "FERPA" but more colloquially referred to as "The Buckley Amendment." This statute grew out of several studies in the early 1970s that found that the record-keeping practices of many elementary and secondary schools failed to protect the privacy interests of students and parents, and gave them little or no voice in crucial decisions affecting their welfare.[28] Although institutions of higher education were included in FERPA almost as an afterthought, it seems clear that the colleges and universities have at least as much if not more power as the lower schools to shape the individual student's future by the records they keep. In a competitive, credentials-conscious society, keeping a clean record, building a resume, and collecting faculty recommendations are the common prerequisites for obtaining admission to desired programs, receiving scholarship assistance, and finding employment opportunities. Although most institutions of higher education have been careful in exercising their record-keeping functions, they are not immune to mistake, bad judgment, sloppiness, or malice in the handling of student records.

In retrospect, some of these past abuses of record-keeping powers now seem extraordinary, as in the case of the 1966 decision by administrators at the University of Michigan to turn over the membership records of several student political organizations to the House Un-American Activities Committee without notifying the students or giving them an opportunity to argue against disclosure.[29] Although the political climate has become less volatile in recent years, problems of government access to student records still arise. The Veterans Administration, for example, reportedly sought access to some universities' files in order to compare the performance of students who were receiving VA assistance with the performance of students who were not.[30] Again, student consent was not requested.

To limit this potential for harm, FERPA and other contemporary privacy laws regard the collection, use, and dissemination of student records as a series of decisions—informal adjudications—that, in practice, determine the individual's access to important rights and benefits. It follows then that the student should be provided the fundamentals of a fair procedure: notice, an opportunity to discover whether there is potentially damaging or inaccurate information in the file, and a chance to dispute or explain harmful items of information. In addition, since university records typically contain sensitive, private information about a student's personal finances, academic performance, and physical, emotional, or disciplinary problems, the student is given a voice in deciding whether the information will be used or disclosed outside the original purposes for which it was collected.

Although these requirements are relatively mild, and the regulations implementing the statute permit the universities considerable flexibility in meeting FERPAs objectives, the act has met strong resistance from the academic community. In essence, the principal objections are twofold: (1) the required procedures are unduly costly to financially hard-pressed institutions, and (2) student access rights will make the records less accurate and useful, primarily by reducing the candor of recommendation letters and other judgmental evaluations. At present there has not been enough experience under FERPA to provide conclusive testing of these arguments. However, available evidence suggests that neither the cost objection nor the candor complaint has much substance.

In considering administrative burdens and costs, one must keep in mind that the early transitional period when regulated institutions are changing their practices to comply with a new statute is likely to be the time when the greatest expense and disruption occur. Yet, when the Privacy Protection Study Commission sought data about these early costs of compliance, it found no substantial evidence that the burdens imposed by FERPA were as severe as the critics claimed.[31] In retrospect, it is perhaps not surprising that the burden feared by FERPAs critics failed to materialize. Even before FERPA, state statutes and judicial decisions had created some student access rights in approximately half of the states,[32] and as a result some institutions may have already developed the required procedures. In any event, FERPA does little more than prescribe good record-keeping practices and minimum standards of fairness in dealing with student files. Any college or university that did experience severe disruption in adjusting to FERPAs requirements probably had inadequate or slipshod record management systems, and should benefit from rationalizing its practices to comply with the statute.

The second standard objection—that recommendation letters will become bland and uninformative if students may see them—is more difficult to evaluate. At the outset there is a real question whether student access to recommendations has been significantly expanded by FERPA. The right to inspect recommendation letters may be waived, and few students are likely to risk the displeasure of the letter-writer by refusing to do so.[33] But even if it could be shown that student access would "chill the candor" of recommendation letters, it is doubtful that this would be a great loss. As anyone knows who has written or read a substantial number of student recommendation letters, they are a notoriously soft and unreliable source of information. If FERPA forces admissions officers and employers to use more objective data in making their decisions, the goals of fairness and accuracy should be served.

The early implementation of FERPA has been neither vigorous nor uniform; nevertheless, there are indications that it is having some beneficial effects. The act reportedly has caused some institutions to clean out stale or unnecessary files, and has provided administrators with a basis for refusing to hand over student files routinely to law enforcement agencies.[34] Beyond its practical impact, FERPA also suggests a symbolic or psychological change in the role of the individual confronting the educational bureaucracy. Instead of being viewed as a "data subject" whose file can be processed, manipulated, and disclosed at will, the student is restored to the status of a unique person who has enforceable rights to control the uses of his or her own information.

While privacy statutes like FERPA are designed to assure fairness in the institution's treatment of the individual, the open-records and open-meetings laws speak primarily to the collective rights of affected groups to monitor and participate in the formulation of institutional policy. Although some public universities may be covered by general state freedom of information, or "sunshine" laws,[35] the movement toward open decision-making in the academic world came largely in response to the demands of students and other internal constituencies in the late 1960s and early 1970s. The rationale for greater disclosure and participatory rights is familiar by now. Openness deters or exposes abuses, brings relevant facts and points of view to the surface before decisions become final, and makes decisions more acceptable to persons and groups who have had an opportunity to participate in the formulation of policy.

As in the privacy debates, the argument has been made that full disclosure chills candor and inhibits frank discussion. Whatever force this argument may have in other contexts, it seems rather implausible when applied to most faculty deliberations. Indeed, some positive benefits may be realized if the prospect of an open meeting forces participants to "do their homework" rather than rambling on extemporaneously, and dampens rhetorical excesses in favor of more realistic problem-solving efforts.

The question of how openness affects the governance of universities and other large institutions is a good deal more complicated than this.

Observers of the many conflicts over access to the meetings and records of the federal bureaucracies have begun to examine in more detail the ways in which openness can alter the dynamics of group decision-making. Some of these commentators have concluded that full disclosure damages the processes by which conflict is mediated and compromise generated.[36] Others have asserted that widespread participation tends to perpetuate the status quo by giving more interest groups an effective veto over proposed actions.[37] The federal experience also suggests that the aggregate costs of a full-disclosure policy can be overwhelming, at least when the institution in question is not trusted by large numbers of its constituents.[38] Implementation of the new information laws is also bringing to the surface the implicit tension between the collective accountability objectives of the openness laws and the individual accountability goals of the privacy statutes. Information that may be useful in monitoring the organization's performance could also be harmful to particular individuals if disclosed to the public, and finding an acceptable balance among the conflicting interests of openness and confidentiality is often a difficult task.

In short, the process of implementing, understanding, and refining the recent information-control statutes is still at a relatively early stage. As is often true of major new legislative programs, both the benefits and the costs of change are sometimes oversold. But underlying the exaggerated claims and criticisms is an important, unfinished social effort to find better means of controlling and humanizing large bureaucratic organizations, including the bureaucracies of higher education.

RULES, REPORTS, AND SANCTIONS

While due process and open government are important aspects of the university's changing relationship with its internal constituencies, the issue of how universities relate to external constituent bodies—predominantly, those bureaucracies which fund and regulate higher education—is a more pressing concern in the minds of most administrators.

To a large and increasing extent, regulatory programs that seek to change university practices are enforced through administrative rules, reporting requirements, and sanctions. The current period of development in administrative law has been called "the age of rulemaking,"[39] and this label seems fully applicable to the regulation of higher education. Requirements for affirmative action in hiring, prohibitions on sex and age discrimination, occupational safety standards, and the recent regulations on fair treatment of the handicapped, all exemplify regulatory programs that operate through a broad delegation of authority to an administrative agency, which then has the responsibility for formulating detailed implementing rules.

In considering the effects of these regulatory programs on the universities it is important to be aware of the differences between the formal paradigm of administratively imposed rules, reporting requirements and sanctions, and the informal processes of bargaining, mediation, and mutual adjustment that give life to the formal model. Much of the hostile reaction among academicians to the process of administrative regulation seems to be directed toward the formal model, which is perceived as a system of inflexible rules imposed by rigid, unresponsive bureaucracies, and backed by devastating sanctions. Such a limited view of the regulatory process can be not only distorted but self-defeating as well. Most regulatory bureaucracies can be moved, but only by those who push hard and in the right places. Knowing where and how to push requires an appreciation of both the formal and informal procedural tools that are available to the regulated.

Rulemaking

Even in its simplest, most discretionary form, administrative rulemaking typically provides affected interests with the rudiments of fair procedure. The agency is required to give interested persons notice and an opportunity to present at least written information and argument before a rule is issued in final form. In many instances, the agency is required by statute to allow considerably more elaborate procedural rights, including formal hearings with the opportunity to cross-examine, and to provide a detailed justification for the rule on the basis of the record it has compiled.[40] Judicial review is commonly available before the rule is enforced, and reviewing courts have been increasingly willing in recent years to probe in depth the factual, legal, and policy bases of administrative rules.

Beneath this formal superstructure, there is often an informal process of information exchange and negotiation between the agency and interested constituencies. An example of informal contacts affecting agency rulemaking is provided by the following description of the drafting of affirmative action rules in 1972:

[A]t the end of July 1972 a 100-page draft of guidelines for the application of the Executive orders . . . to institutions of higher education was prepared [by the U.S. Department of Health, Education and Welfare] and sent to some two dozen university officials for their personal review and their comment by mid-August, as it was hoped that a guidelines document could be published by the opening of the academic year in September.

Some of the university officials who received the document presented to the appropriate officials in the Department of Labor their strong objections to parts of the HEW draft. The Director of Federal Contract Compliance in the Department of Labor has to approve any regulations [of this nature] . . . .

The Department of Labor officials, recognizing that the 100-page draft was unnecessarily detailed, ambiguous, and intrusive, instructed HEW to develop a new draft cut down perhaps to one-third the size, tightly organized and objectively written. . . .

. . . HEW issued its guidelines in October 1972. For the most part, these guidelines follow the specifications stated by the Department of Labor.[41]

Prepublication negotiations of this nature are a common feature of the rulemaking process because they can be beneficial to both the regulators and the regulated. The agency on the one hand typically knows less about the operations of the regulated industry and the possible consequences of the rule than industry members do; and most bureaucrats have an aversion to surprises, especially those that may bring public or political criticism. For the regulated parties, on the other hand, the informal give-and-take with agency representatives provides an opportunity to shape the agency's thinking before positions have solidified.

The effectiveness of the regulated industry at the informal levels of decision-making may depend in large measure on its willingness and ability to use the more formal procedural rights that are available to it. In most fields of economic regulations, government agencies have learned the hard way that a failure to respond to legitimate objections from the regulated industry can lead to bitter, protracted hearings at the agency level, and judicial reversals of the rules that are finally issued. The academic community has seemed reluctant to resort to formal procedures and lawsuits, and as a result may have less leverage in the informal stages of rulemaking than it could have. However, this condition may be changing as the regulatory process becomes more familiar and pervasive in higher education.

Reporting Requirements

When the regulatory process shifts from rulemaking to the enforcement phase, another set of dynamics comes into play. Many contemporary regulatory systems, including the major federal programs affecting higher education, rely heavily on reporting requirements which empower the agency to specify the nature and format of information that must be filed by the regulated industry. The "utilization analyses," "goals and timetables," and other paperwork required under the affirmative action program are familiar examples of this approach. From the government's perspective, reporting requirements have obvious advantages over alternative enforcement strategies such as waiting for complainants to report violations or sending investigators out to examine the activities of particular institutions. Regular reports can provide a detailed, systematic view, extended over time, of the compliance activities of the regulated industry, and identify targets for more intensive enforcement activities. Self-reporting can also provide more accurate information at less total cost than having government investigators who are outsiders collect the data. And, perhaps most important of all, reporting requirements can shift a large part of the costs of compliance from government to the regulated industry. Of course, the cost-shifting feature is the reason why reporting requirements often are distasteful and burdensome to the regulated industry, and as a result these provisions are a frequent point of conflict in administrative regulation.

The formal legal system generally confers broad information-gathering power on the administrative agency. The statutes permit considerable discretion in prescribing the content and timing of reports and in obtaining access to records. The person or organization that is ordered to report may be able to obtain some form of court review, but the scope of this review tends to be quite limited. At the informal level, however, the realities are somewhat different. Even if a court battle over reporting requirements is won by the agency, the delays and other costs associated with litigation can slow or cripple an enforcement program. Moreover, the agencies are accountable not only to the courts but also to legislatures and executive officials, and these political overseers are often very responsive to the regulated industry's claims that they are being subject to unnecessary paperwork. But the regulated cannot be too intransigent since resistance creates costs and risks, including the loss of good will and support that can result from appearing to be an opponent of the underlying goals of the regulatory program. Few university administrators, for example, would want to appear hostile to the ideal of equal opportunity for minorities, women, or the handicapped—a reputation that might well follow from vociferous opposition to reporting requirements.

When these conflicting pressures exist, neither the regulators nor the regulated can escalate the conflict without risk to themselves. Often, both sides give a little, and a compromise set of reporting requirements is worked out. There is at least some indirect evidence that this is happening in the administration of reporting requirements applicable to the universities. While educators have been complaining about the stifling paperwork burden associated with federal programs such as affirmative action, civil rights advocates have sharply criticized the Higher Education Division of HEWs Office for Civil Rights on the ground that it has failed to impose on the universities reporting requirements which are comparable to those demanded of other federal contractors.[42]

Even when the agencies are willing to compromise on reporting requirements, there remains a considerable (if poorly documented) cost burden for the universities to absorb. Part of this burden may result from overlapping, piecemeal, regulatory programs that are administered sometimes inconsistently by different agencies, or by different subunits of the same agency.[43] At the same time, many academic observers suspect that the mandatory reports include information that is irrelevant or misleading, and that the quantities of data demanded cannot even be digested by the regulators.[44] As President Robben Fleming of the University of Michigan asserted: "[T]he cost and effort [of compiling information] might be justified if it could be demonstrated that it is productive. On the contrary, it is evident that enforcement agencies are not staffed to examine and analyze the mountains of material which they are accumulating. Unless the whole procedure is a form of punishment . . . it is hard to see what really useful purpose it is serving."[45]

While these problems are real, they are not incurable. In large measure, they can be traced to conditions such as understaffing in the regulatory agency, and enforcement officials' unfamiliarity with the operations and mores of the university. Another aggravating factor is the use of reporting requirements developed to deal with hiring practices in industrial enterprises which do not fit smoothly into the rather different recruitment and employment practices found in higher education. Given the inherent flexibility of the administrative process, however, it should be possible to work out satisfactory solutions for many of these problems in the reporting requirements if the regulated seize the opportunity to influence the regulators.

Enforcement Actions

The final stage in this paradigm of the regulatory process is enforcement against those who have violated the rules. When formal accusations are made against a member of the regulated industry and sanctions are threatened, the full spectrum of due process rights to notice and a fair hearing generally comes into play, and judicial review is usually available if the accused is found guilty at the administrative level. Perhaps the most significant feature of the formal sanctioning process, however, is the fact that it is rarely used in many regulatory programs. This seems especially true when sanctions involve the termination of large-scale federal funding arrangements, a situation which encompasses many of the regulatory programs that affect higher education. Even the affirmative action program, which has been highly controversial since the 1972 amendments to the regulations, has not generated a substantial amount of formal enforcement activity. Indeed, it was not until 1977 that reports were published describing the first formal enforcement proceeding against a university for violation of the executive order, and even then the administrative decision was not final.[46] Minority and women's rights advocates have complained bitterly about HEWs tendency to negotiate with the universities over compliance rather than to take formal enforcement action,[47] and at times they have resorted to lawsuits against the agency in an effort to compel more vigorous enforcement of equal opportunity rules.[48]

The reasons behind the agencies' reluctance to employ the formal sanctioning apparatus can be found in the sanctions themselves. When the principal or only sanction is a total termination of federal funding, or a flat ban on future grants and contracts, the sanctions may actually be too devastating to use. A funding cutoff could threaten the survival of even a major university, could harm innocent students and faculty not responsible for the violation, and could prevent the government from procuring needed products or services from the offending institution. These sweeping sanctions are, as one knowledgeable observer put it, "clumsy and overpotent,"[49] and it is small wonder that the regulators will not lightly invoke them. By the same token, many university administrators may regard any possibility of a federal fund cutoff, however slight, a risk they cannot accept.

These incentives to avoid formal proceedings doubtless tend to compel bargaining and a search for compromise solutions, but they may also generate needless friction and cynicism among parties to the transaction. Enforcement officials may feel that there is no credible response they can make to violations that do not merit the severest sanctions; educators may feel that they are powerless to resist the demands of enforcement officials even when the university can make a relatively strong case for its position; and the intended beneficiaries of the regulatory program may feel that enforcement is a sham because the statutory sanctions are never imposed. A more realistic range of flexible sanctions could improve relationships among the agency and its constituencies and provide a more structured context for the processes of negotiation and compromise.

The general outline of the regulatory process that emerges from this paradigm is a system in which change often takes place incrementally through bargaining and compromise, under the formal structure of legal and administrative procedures. This environment may be uncomfortable for many educators. By training and temperament, academicians tend to prefer clarity to ambiguity, and they value principled, reasoned decisions over bargained or compromised outcomes.[50] But adapting to a system of regulation does not inevitably result in a surrender to raw pragmatism, unrelieved by any aspiration or fidelity to higher values. Regulation of higher education, like most other fields of public administration, involves efforts to reconcile, in particular settings, the conflicts among important, widely shared values such as academic freedom and equality of opportunity, fairness to the individual, and educational quality. If these goals are kept in sight, a process that leaves room for negotiation and accommodation among contending interests may be the surest method of producing social change.

CONCLUSION

As the influence of regulatory procedures, programs, and techniques spreads throughout higher education, there may be fundamental changes not only in the way the university interacts with the outside world but also in the way it governs itself internally. University administrators will increasingly come into direct contact with the various regulatory bureaucracies. Dealing effectively with this new set of external constituencies will require further development of capacities and skills that most administrators already possess to some degree. Perhaps most important is sensitivity to changing social needs and demands. Regulatory intervention is likely to be most intrusive and disruptive when the institution being regulated has failed to adapt to the evolving concerns of the society. Administrators would be wise to develop a more sophisticated understanding of the workings of the regulatory process, including the various procedural tools and techniques that can be used to affect agency decisions. And they must be willing to use these tools in appropriate circumstances—to bargain hard when there is room for reasonable accommodation and to resort to the courts when litigation is necessary.

The regulatory presence is likely to be felt not only in more frequent contacts between university administrators and government regulators but also in the relationship evolving between the universities and intermediary organizations such as the American Council on Education (ACE). In many areas of economic regulation, the enactment of regulatory programs has resulted in increased powers and responsibilities among the trade or professional associations that represent the collective interests of the regulated industry. This often occurs because a single, central association can develop influence and resources that its dispersed members can rarely match. With a full-time, specialized staff the association can master the intricacies of regulatory programs more completely than an administrator or manager who devotes only part of his or her attention to the task. It can also bring together reliable information about general trends and conditions within the sector of the economy it represents, and its position as a general representative of the industry gives the association's views more weight and authority. Through continuous monitoring of the regulatory bureaucracies, a central association often gains the important advantages of access and timing; it can reach the key decision-makers with data and argument at a time when regulatory policy is still in flux and amenable to change. In short, the greater economy and effectiveness of central representation often lead the regulated to delegate the principal responsibility for protecting their interests in the regulatory process to the association.

There are already some signs that higher education is following the patterns set by the regulated industries in their dealings with government agencies. The American Council on Education and the more specialized professional and academic associations are frequent, effective participants in the regulatory process. The *Chronicle of Higher Education* covers government regulatory stories as intensively as many industry trade journals do. And the capture of administrative agencies by the regulated industry seems to be well advanced in the field of higher education. Two university chancellors were appointed recently to the ranking positions dealing with higher education in the federal bureaucracy—Assistant Secretary for Education of the Department of HEW and U.S. Commissioner of Education.[51] At about the same time, a congressional report criticized the Federal Advisory Committee for Higher Educational Equal Employment Opportunity Programs on the grounds that it was dominated by university administrators and tended to make recommendations that weakened the enforcement of equal opportunity laws.[52] In addition, higher education spokespersons have recorded notable lobbying victories such as the congressional amendment of FERPA only one month after the original "Buckley Amendment" went into effect.[53]

If these developments do foreshadow an enhanced role for intermediary organizations such as ACE, there may be significant changes in the individual universities' relationships to these associations. One possible consequence is increasing pressure for member institutions to support the position advocated by the association. A dissident university may find itself in the doubly disadvantageous position not only of having to represent itself without the resources and expertise of the association, but also of having to argue against the weight and authority of an establishment viewpoint. The associations, by virtue of their specialized knowledge and their strategic position between government and academe, may also become more active in shaping collective policy positions, rather than being simply a reflection of the desires of their constituents.[54] If the power and influence of the associations do grow in this fashion, the universities may find themselves much more deeply involved in questions of who will lead these organizations and what policies and priorities they will adopt.

Increasing contact with the regulatory process may also bring changes in the internal governance of the universities. The twin pressures for increased procedural fairness to internal constituencies and for greater accountability to outside regulators should continue to expand the administrative workload, requiring more administrators and inflating the costs of administration. Internal administrative stresses may be magnified as universities juggle personnel and organizational structures to meet these enlarged demands. And efforts to shift some of the costs back to the regulatory bodies that are imposing the procedural requirements also seem likely. The recent disputes over the adequacy of government reimbursement of indirect costs to universities receiving research grants may well be just the preliminary round in an extended struggle over who will ultimately bear the burden of regulation.

As the administrative work of the universities grows in size and complexity, there may also be changes in the kinds of people who are involved in academic administration. In this emerging regulatory environment, faculty members who have specialized in the humanities or the hard sciences may find it more and more difficult to move into administration; by contrast, teachers who have trained in fields related to administration—management, law, policy studies, and the like—may have a relative advantage. Ultimately, as a result of the continuing pressures of specialization and workload, much of the work of academic administration may be delegated to individuals who are making a career in the field, and who have only minimal direct involvement in the teaching and research missions of the university.

If such a trend does materialize, it will have high potential for destructive conflict within the universities. In any large bureaucracy tension often arises between line and staff personnel; in the university these tensions may be enhanced by the unremitting hostility many faculty members feel toward anything that even faintly resembles regimentation or bureaucratic red tape. The university administrators, who speak the same language as the external regulators and consider at least some of their demands legitimate, may become the lightning rod for faculty distrust and contempt of the modern bureaucratic state.

In its extreme form, such distrust can breed conspiracy theories of petty officials inside and outside the universities plotting to subvert academic values. A Carnegie Commission study of federal antibias regulation verges close at times to this extreme:

> HEW enforcement officers in some regions seek numerical goals and timetables by department or "hiring unit," a key element in affirmative action programs, including for faculty. . . . The authority structure they tend to favor conflicts with the collegial or faculty system of shared responsibility in decision-making by mature teacher-scholars. The HEW enforcement officers, interested in certain results more than in procedures to assure the best professional judgments, seem desirous of enhancing the authority of a university's newly appointed equal employment officers and coordinators, who, for the most part, have not been drawn from the faculty. . . .
>
> [T]hrough their power to approve or disapprove affirmative action plans, HEW enforcement officials are, either consciously or unconsciously, attempting to alter the structure of authority and governance in universities in line with the industrial model. . . . In doing so, they are tending to undermine faculty self-government. . . .[55]

A more moderate variant of this perspective sees the university administrators as well-intentioned but misguided, incorrigible "bureaucratic outsiders" whose overzealous efforts to save the university may actually destroy it. In this view, adoption of the bureaucratic style—devotion to rational planning, procedural regularity and fairness, reasoned decisions, efficiency and accountability—"does not serve to insulate the University from outside pressures to control it; rather, it cuts channels to transmit those pressures inward."[56]

Explicit in these critiques, and implicit in others, are questions not only about who will control higher education or how control will be exercised but also about the ends that will be sought by those using the various regulatory techniques and processes. Bureaucracy and its procedures are tools that can be used wisely or poorly, in the service of many purposes. If used sensitively, administrative procedures can harness the collective energies of large organizations to achieve desired goals effectively, responsibly, and humanely. But procedures and process values can become ends in themselves, a repressive or stultifying force, if they are not held subordinate to primary values. Experience suggests that the organization or institution which lacks a clearly defined, widely shared sense of mission or identity is most vulnerable to strangulation by red tape; and it may be that much of the anguished reaction to government regulation springs from deep-seated doubts that the universities really have this shared sense of mission.

In recent decades, the traditional ideal of the university as a collegium of interacting scholars and students dedicated to a common core of academic values and sharing a common language of discourse has seemed increasingly remote and unattainable. To some observers, centripetal pressures—narrow disciplinary specialization, the demands and inducements of outside funding sources, the pull of instrumental and vocational interests—have tended to transform the university into a "multiversity," a place that, in Clark Kerr's description, often appears to be no more than "a mechanism held together by administrative rules and powered by money."[57]

These critiques can be faulted for romanticizing the past and overstating the present crisis, but nevertheless they raise serious questions that go to the heart of the evolving relationship between government and higher education. If, as we believe, colleges and universities can succeed in articulating to themselves and their constituencies the goals, values, and functions that are fundamentally important to their role in contemporary society, then the increasing interactions with the regulatory process may be as much an opportunity as a threat. But it is essential to approach this task in the right spirit and to avoid what Gerald Grant and David Riesman have called "fantasies of omnipotence" and "fantasies of total powerlessness" while trying to discover "what kinds of human quality can be nurtured in a college setting that can support the rationality necessary for a technological order along with, rather than in antagonism to, the more contemplative and expressive values."[58]

NOTES

1. Chronicle of Higher Education, June 23, 1975, at 1, cols. 2–4.

2. Harvard University Gazette, June 13, 1975, at 1, col. 2.

3. O'Neill, *God and Government at Yale: The Limits of Federal Regulation of Higher Education*, 44 U. Cin. L. Rev. 525 (1975).

4. *Id.*

5. *See, e.g.*, Oaks, *A Private University Looks at Government Regulation*, 4 J. Coll. & Univ. Law 1 (1976). *But see* Jenkins, *Regulation of Colleges and Universities Under the Guaranteed Student Loan Program*, *id.* at 13.

6. Some commentators see a measure of poetic justice in the application to higher education of regulatory programs and techniques that were originally designed or advocated by academicians. Former Solicitor General Robert Bork has been quoted as espousing this view:

"The academic world has been actively hostile to the claims of other non-governmental institutions to autonomy in the name of greater efficiency that benefits society," he said.

"The result is not only that many today take pleasure in the plight of academics forced to swallow their own medicine, but also the public philosophy of dispersed authority has been undermined and ridiculed by intellectuals who now invoke it for their own benefit.

"It should not come as a surprise if that invocation is met with a smile."

Chronicle of Higher Education, Dec. 20, 1976, at 5, col. 5.

7. *See* Fleming, Chapter 2 *supra*.

8. *See generally* Wright, *The Constitution on Campus*, 22 Vand. L. Rev. 1027; D. Hornby, *Higher Education Admission Law Service* (1973).

9. Interestingly, little attention has yet been paid to the process relied upon by universities in drawing such standards and procedures. If the federal experience in rulemaking is instructive, that too will become a focus of interest and searching scrutiny. *See generally* Hamilton, *Procedures for the Adoption of Rules of General Applicability: The Need for Procedural Innovation in Administrative Rulemaking*, 60 Calif. L. Rev. 1276; Wright, *The Courts and the Rulemaking Process: The Limits of Judicial Review*, 59 Cornell L. Rev. 375 (1974). Williams, *"Hybrid Rulemaking" Under the Administrative Procedure Act: A Legal and Empirical Analysis*, 42 U. Chi. L. Rev. 401 (1975); Pedersen, *Formal Records and Informal Rulemaking*, 85 Yale L.J. 38 (1975); Friendly, *"Some Kind of a Hearing,"* 123 U. Pa. L. Rev. 1267 (1975).

10. *See generally*, Gellhorn & Hornby, *Constitutional Limitations on Admissions Procedures and Standards*, 60 Va. L. Rev. 975, 979–98 (1974).

11. 400 U.S. 160.

12. *See* Hornby, *supra* note 8, at §§ 110–14, 165. Occasional cases have extended this list to include Fourth Amendment protections against unreasonable searches and seizures. *See* Buss, *The Fourth Amendment and Searches of Students in Public Schools*, 59 Iowa L. Rev. 739 (1974). And, of course, the traditional forms of invidious discrimination because of race, religion, or national origin are forbidden on the campus as elsewhere.

13. It is also worth noting that the courts are increasingly cautious in their extension and application of these basic concepts into new areas. There is, in other words, room for universities to experiment and try new approaches. Only when such efforts are inadequate are the courts likely to step in.

14. 294 F.2d 150 (5th Cir. 1961), *cert. denied*, 368 U.S. 930.

15. *See generally* Goss v. Lopez, 419 U.S. 565.

16. And even the erosion now occurring at the elementary school level— where occasional opportunities are available to question classification decisions—is seemingly limited to two minimal procedural requirements, namely, uniformity of application and fair administration of the regulations.

17. 411 U.S. 1.

18. 81 Stat. § 6, *codified in* U.S.C. § 552.

19. 88 Stat. 1564.

20. 90 Stat. 1246, *codified in* 5 U.S.C. § 552b.

21. 86 Stat. 770.

22. 88 Stat. 1905, *codified in* 5 U.S.C. § 552a (Supp. V).

23. 15 U.S.C. §§ 1681–1681t.

24. 88 Stat. 1511.

25. 88 Stat. 1521.

26. The Privacy Protection Study Commission, Personal Privacy in an Information Society (1977).

27. 20 U.S.C. § 1232g (Supp. V).

28. *See generally* Privacy Protection Study Commission, *supra* note 26, at 411–13; Recent Development, *The Buckley Amendment: Opening School Files for Student and Parental Review*, 24 Catholic U.L. Rev. 588, 594 n.38 (1975).

29. *See* N.Y Times, Dec. 13, 1966, at 20, col. 4.

30. Privacy Protection Study Commission, *supra* note 26, at 409.

31.

In response to the Commission's direct request for data on the cost of implementing FERPA, only one institution produced evidence of extra expenditures. Its estimate, after careful analysis, was that FERPA cost about one extra dollar per year per student and, in doing the analysis, it discovered several places in which the flexibility FERPA allows would enable it to cut even that cost without detriment to the individual student. Had the cost of implementing FERPA been as great as the rhetoric would suggest, the Commission's request for data would surely have produced budgeting and planning documents reflecting the costs from institutions that had found them to be burdensome. While there are obviously some costs incurred in implementing the law—an extra page or two of printing, an extra form for those who wish directory information withheld, and the cost of discussions with faculty, staff, and administrators—it seems safe to infer that they are insignificant.

Id. at 418.

32. *See* Cudlipp, *The Family Educational Rights and Privacy Act Two Years Later*, 11 U. Richmond L. Rev. 33, 34–35 (1976).

33. *See* Privacy Protection Study Commission, *supra* note 26, at 424.

34. Cudlipp, *supra* note 32, at 39.

35. *See generally* Shurtz, *The University in the Sunshine: Application of the Open Meeting Laws to the University Setting*, 5 J. Law & Educ. 453 (1976).

36. *See* Perrit & Wilkinson, *Open Advisory Committees and the Political Process: The Federal Advisory Committee Act After Two Years*, 63 Geo. L.J. 725, 739–42 (1975).

37. *See* Cleveland, *How Do You Get Everybody in on the Act and Still Get Some Action? reprinted in* 120 Cong. Rec. § 19, at 455–57 (daily ed. Nov. 18, 1974).

38. The U.S. Department of Justice, parent agency of the FBI, spent more than half a million man-hours responding to requests for information in 1976, and at one point the agency's backlog in processing requests extended for several years.

39. Wright, *The Courts and the Rulemaking Process: The Limits of Judicial Review*, 59 Cornell L. Rev. 375 (1974).

40. For a discussion of the various forms of administrative rulemaking procedures in the federal system, *see* Hamilton, *Procedures for the Adoption of Rules of General Applicability: The Need for Procedural Innovation in Administrative Rulemaking*, 60 Cal. L. Rev. 1277 (1972).

41. R. Lester, *Antibias Regulation of Universities, reprinted in* Hearings on Federal Higher Education Programs Institutional Eligibility, 93d Cong., 2d Sess., pt. 2B at 1006, 1072–73 (1974).

42. *See, e.g.*, The Federal Civil Rights Enforcement Effort—1974, Vol. III, at 275–81, 289 (A Report of the United States Commission on Civil Rights, Jan. 1975).

43. *See, e.g.*, Vetter, *Affirmative Action in Faculty Employment Under Executive Order 11246*, in Hearings on Federal Higher Education Programs Institutional Eligibility, 93d Cong., 2d Sess., pt. 2A, at 357, 368–75 (1974).

44. *See generally* Lester, *supra* note 41.

45. Hearings on Federal Higher Education Programs, *supra* note 43, at 93–94.

46. Chronicle of Higher Education, Feb. 22, 1977, at 11, col. 1.

47. *See, e.g.*, Hearings on Federal Higher Education Programs, *supra* note 43, at 326 (*Statement of Mordeca Jane Pollock, Employment Compliance Task Force, National Organization for Women*): "HEW has repeatedly neglected to initiate enforcement proceedings when it has found violations by colleges and universities   Instead, it has routinely elected to pursue protracted negotiations, which sometimes last several years, and which ultimately lead to no relief for victims of discrimination.") *See also id.* at 73 (*Statement of Peter E. Holmes, Director, Office for Civil Rights, DHEW*).

48. Adams v. Richardson, 480 F.2d 1159, discussed in The Federal Civil Rights Enforcement Effort—1974, Vol. III, *supra* note 42, at 256–64.

49. Vetter, *supra* note 43, at 359.

50. A classic articulation of this perspective is Theodore Lowi's chapter on *Liberal Jurisprudence*, in The End of Liberalism 125–56 (paper ed. 1969).

51. Chronicle of Higher Education, Jan. 24, 1977, at 1, col. 3. The report further notes: "President Carter and members of his Cabinet have appointed academicians to a number of top level federal posts, despite earlier fears that the academic community might be shunned by the new administration." *Id.* at 10, col. 1.

52. Chronicle of Higher Education, Feb. 22, 1977, at 11, col. 1.

53. *School Files for Student and Parental Review*, 24 Catholic U.L. Rev. 588, 588–89 (1975).

54. *Cf.* L. Dexter, *How Organizations Are Represented in Washington* 103 (1969) [emphasis removed]:

> Many clients and employers do not like, naturally enough, the idea that people whom they have hired are guiding and educating them. Nevertheless, a good many clients are educated or guided. . . .
>   . . . The most important service of Washington representatives to

clients and employers is teaching the latter to live with the government and in the society. That is, Washington representatives instruct a good many clients how to adapt, accommodate, and adjust.

55. R. Lester, *supra* note 41, at 1118–19.

56. The language is taken, admittedly somewhat out of context, from a dialogue concerning a draft academic plan for the State University of New York at Buffalo. SUNYAB Reporter, Jan. 13, 1977, at 8, cols. 1–2. However, the statement from which the quotations come seems to reflect a broad underlying suspicion of bureaucratic approaches to the governance of universities, and in this respect probably exemplifies the attitude of many who are involved in higher education.

57. C. Kerr, The Uses of the University 20 (paper ed. 1972).

58. Grant & Reisman, *An Ecology of Academic Reform*, 104 Daedalus 166, 185–86 (Winter, 1975).

Chapter 4

The Academic Industry—
A Dangerous Premise

Estelle A. Fishbein

In Chapter 3, Professors Gellhorn and Boyer examine the procedural constraints and requirements imposed on higher education by the federal government, and explore the impact on universities of these obligations (both legislatively and judicially inspired) to assess their course. As can be expected of lawyers, after surveying the same ground we reach quite different opinions.

In serving as legal counsel to a university, I have found no resistance to the idea that discretion ought to be exercised responsibly and fairly. In fact it is my impression that administrators tend to make extraordinary efforts to be fair. But the due process requirements that the courts have imposed upon public universities have had an unfortunate consequence, namely, that today students and faculty alike appear to have a legal cause of action no matter how minor the dispute. Almost every exercise of discretion is thus escalated to the level of a constitutional issue, and there is commonly a race to the door of the federal courthouse by every dissatisfied party to an administrative decision. In other words, everything becomes a federal case. As a result, matters that earlier were ordinary problems of public campus administration are today legal confrontations. And relationships between students and administrators, between students and faculty, and between faculty and administrators become increasingly adversarial. Students who are terminated in a Ph.D. program are still likely to discuss the matter with the department chairman—only now through a lawyer. And sometimes they bypass the chairman altogether and go directly to the university's attorney.

This is an appalling development. Although courts generally have been reluctant to become involved in the review of a dismissal for academic deficiency, there are disturbing indications that the judgments by faculty regarding academic performance and intellectual capability also may be subjected to due process requirements, as is the rule in disciplinary dismissals. In *Greenhill v. Bailey*, for example, the Eighth Circuit Court of Appeals directed the University of Iowa Medical School to provide a hearing to a student who was dismissed on grounds of academic deficiencies, since that dismissal imposed a stigma that affected his freedom to take advantage of alternative opportunities at other medical schools.[1] Similarly, in *Board of Curators of the University of Missouri v. Horowitz* the Supreme Court has consented to decide whether the Eighth Circuit Court was correct in ordering the School of Medicine at the University of Missouri at Kansas City to afford notice and hearing to a medical student who was expelled because of poor clinical competence, inability to accept criticism, poor peer and patient relationships, and bad personal hygiene.[2]

It is regrettable that so many aspects of life at public universities have been remolded in a legalistic, highly procedural fashion. It means, of course, that the administrator in the public university must undertake his or her daily tasks in the company of a lawyer since everything that is done constitutes state action and subjects the administrator to personal liability under 42 U.S.C. 1983. And that word has spread among those engaged in the administration of public universities, with predictably adverse results to their morale. Although Professors Gellhorn and Boyer do not discuss the distinction between public and private universities with regard to due process requirements, there is no question that one of the attractions of private universities today is the relative freedom from observance of the technicalities of due process, and the fact that officers and administrators of private institutions are less exposed to personal, legal liability than are their public counterparts.

However, the contention with which I most strongly disagree is that the larger role of government in university affairs has not been seriously detrimental, and higher education's reaction to the current wave of government regulation "as if it were as dangerous as the McCarthyism of the fifties" is unwarranted hysteria. Gellhorn and Boyer have badly understated the current role of government and its attendant bureaucracies in the internal affairs of universities. Government regulation is not the "wave" the authors describe it to be; it is rather more akin to a tidal wave. Such regulation is vastly *more* dangerous than the McCarthyism of the fifties, and higher education's reaction has been too little, too late, too cautious, and far too polite.

Professors Gellhorn and Boyer appear to accept unquestioningly the premise that a university is simply another industrial organization like GM, GE, and Bethlehem Steel. Their view accurately reflects the prevailing attitude of legislators and bureaucrats today, and when one hears it stated so often one is easily lulled into accepting it. But it is a dangerous premise and must be questioned repeatedly, resisted unfailingly, and consistently discarded.

Many distinctions immediately come to mind. Unlike commercial industrial organizations, universities do not owe their existence to the profit motive. Although universities are ever in pursuit of a balanced budget and an excess of income over expenses, their surpluses are not likely to be devoted to ventures yielding the highest dollar return consistent with safety. Rather, universities are likely to invest any surplus they may realize at little or no interest in the most speculative risk possible—their students.

Essentially, however, the distinction between the corporate organization calling itself a university and the counterpart organization within the business and industrial complex lies in the fact that universities have a special relationship to the First Amendment not commonly shared by commercial industrial enterprises. For the university, much like the press, is a custodian of the most fragile of our civil liberties, namely, freedom of speech and thought. In that light, universities are the nation's most precious resource, a repository of our intellectual heritage and a source of future intellectual growth and development. Manufacturers and retail establishments may be regulated and constricted, yet the business of production and buying and selling can still go on. But if regulation of the university inhibits inquiry, if it suppresses the free exercise of intellectual judgment and the responsible exercise of discretion, then the business of the university is concluded.

Title IX, Title VII, the statutes prohibiting discrimination on the basis of age and handicap, the Equal Pay Act, the Buckley Amendment, and the Health Professions Educational Assistance Act of 1976 all intrude into internal institutional affairs to an alarming degree, greatly proscribing the institution's right to select and deal with its own students, its faculty, and its curriculum. The Buckley Amendment furnishes a good example in particular of the federal government's intrusion into the minutiae which is part of the daily operation of a university. Inasmuch as the legislation was enacted without benefit of prior public hearing, no attention was given to whether access to educational records in institutions of higher education and the maintenance of the confidentiality of such records are appropriate matters for federal concern, federal legislation, and federal superintendence. No responsible study had demonstrated that students generally have been adversely affected by the manner in which educational records have been maintained by colleges. Indeed, had an inquiry been made, the drafters of the legislation would have discovered that most institutions of higher education already went to considerable length to preserve the confidentiality of student records, yet to disclose to the student academic information in the records he or she had a legitimate need to know. Institutional policies on this subject, although they might differ in minor respects, were the result of institutional experience, academic judgments, and common sense. Indeed, for some years prior to the passage of the Buckley Amendment, there existed a Guide to the Release of Information About Students. The guide was developed by the American Association of Collegiate Registrars and Admissions Officers, a professional organization active since 1910 that counseled institutions of higher education to formulate policies regarding both the information that becomes part of a student's permanent educational record and the conditions of its disclosure. The guide's introduction advised that, "This policy should reflect a reasonable balance between the obligation of the institution for the growth and welfare of the student and its responsibilities to society." Higher education's quarrel with the Buckley Amendment and the accompanying regulations is that evidently no consideration was given to striking a reasonable balance between these interests and responsibilities. The result of that neglect has been to harm institutions by imposing unnecessary and onerous governmental regulation in an area where there had been no demonstrable problem of appreciable dimensions and, more importantly, to harm those who were to be the beneficiaries of the new legislation, namely, students.

Professors Gellhorn and Boyer speak of the Buckley Amendment (more precisely, the amendment to the Buckley Amendment) as an instance when "educational interests have also been known to mount intensive and successful lobbying efforts." The example is not particularly persuasive since the changes effected were of no great consequence and hardly reduced the burdens of the legislation on colleges. Probably the most significant changes were those denying students access to financial information provided by parents, permitting schools to hold confidential all letters of recommendation placed in a student's file prior to January 1, 1975, and providing for waiver by students of the right to examine letters of recommendation. Educational interests have little reason to boast of their "successful" lobbying efforts where the Buckley Amendment is concerned!

With the Health Professions Educational Assistance Act of 1976 (P.L. 94-484), Congress has managed new levels of encroachment onto the academic turf; this legislation may be an indication of things to come. It decrees that, as a condition of receiving capitation grants (which have been provided since 1971 to assist professional schools in meeting the particularly high cost of educating health professionals) medical schools must admit as transferees American medical students studying abroad who have completed two years and have passed Part I of the National Board examinations. These students must be admitted regardless of their academic qualifications and places of residence. In short, the federal government has removed authority and control over admissions from the medical school faculty. Happily, vigorous opposition by schools of medicine and a decision by several to forego grant monies rather than surrender the right to apply normal academic criteria to applicants, resulted in a recent significant amendment of the statute: under the Health Professions Education Amendments of 1977, although schools must increase their enrollments on a temporary one-year basis by 5 percent, they no longer are precluded from applying normal admissions and academic criteria.

The statute, moreover, intrudes deeply into the autonomy which professional schools previously enjoyed over their own curricula. Hereafter, all medical schools must devote a certain percentage of their residency training programs to primary care—that is, to pediatrics, family medicine, and internal medicine. Schools of pharmacy are required to have their students take a program entitled "clinical pharmacy" which includes four specific curricular components. Schools of dentistry are required to increase their first-year enrollments by at least ten students, or to have all students participate for at least six weeks in a program of clinical training located in a remote site or in medically underserved areas. Again, the legislation specifies several elements of the curriculum; but not content simply to prescribe dental curriculum, the legislation also mandates that faculty be appointed from among practicing dentists.

In my view, the dean and faculty of the Johns Hopkins School of Medicine are more qualified to determine the curriculum of the school of medicine, to judge which applicants show the greatest promise for medical careers, and to establish the criteria of faculty appointment than is the Congress or the secretary of HEW. Certainly the Johns Hopkins School of Medicine, together with its sister schools across the nation, have managed to make successful judgments in these traditional areas for quite some time without federal guidance.

Federal agencies are so ill-equipped and uncomfortable in regulating the university that, regardless of the objective of the regulatory activity, they have depended on trial and error in fashioning regulatory policy. In an incisive article concerning Title IX and athletics in the November 1976 issue of *Change Magazine*, George LaNoue comments that HEWs use of trial and error as an enforcement mechanism as well has invited bureaucratic mischief. "Dependence on the 'reasonableness' of the policemen is an intolerable way to enforce a civil rights law."[3] The alarming aspect of federal regulation of education is that the trial and error mechanism is characteristic of the federal regulatory presence on campus. A marvelous example, almost Kafkaesque, is the Department of Labor's bumbling efforts to apply the Equal Pay Act to universities and colleges.

The Equal Pay Act prohibits salary discrimination on the basis of sex, and requires employers to pay equal wages to persons who are performing jobs that require equal skill, effort, and responsibility that are performed under similar working conditions. Differentials are permitted if they are based on merit, seniority, or any factor other than sex. There is little difficulty in applying this law and its salutory principle to the industrial sector or even to the university where nonacademic employees are concerned. A bus driver is a bus driver, and a department secretary may be likened to other department secretaries. But by their very nature scholars are not interchangeable, just as actresses, musicians, and poets are not interchangeable. The university, when hiring a faculty member, is looking for quality of mind, promise of productivity, and singularity of contribution. A scholar is not and cannot be judged by quantitative and visible standards.

The Department of Labor has never issued regulations or guidelines regarding the application of the Equal Pay Act to faculty pay in higher education. No definitive policy statement has ever been issued. This, however, has not prevented the Department of Labor from bringing suit against Northeastern University, charging violation of the Equal Pay Act. The complaint filed in federal court by the government is skeletal and conclusory despite the fact that it followed a two-year investigation. Finally, the department selected fifty-seven cases of alleged sex discrimination in salary levels, not one of which involved alleged inequity within the university's academic departmental structure. Labor is apparently contending that it can select matchmates for female faculty members across department lines (one professor being likened to another), although nowhere has any statute or regulation given notice to universities that faculty in all deparments must be paid the same, nor has any definitive policy statement been issued from the department setting forth criteria to be used in equating faculty in the various disciplines. Quite recently the American Council on Education demanded of the Department of Labor, under authority of the Freedom of Information Act, the Department's policy memoranda and instructions to its enforcement personnel concerning application of the Equal Pay Act to faculty employees in universities; the Council also sought reports of all studies dealing with the application of the Act. The Department's reply indicated there were no documents of such a nature. Nevertheless, Northeastern University, in its negotiation of an out of court settlement, is being asked by the government for a consent decree that would include an admission of discrimination.

Professors Gellhorn and Boyer's optimistic suggestion that education is in the process of "capturing" the regulatory agencies is not persuasive. In support of their position, they observe that two university chancellors have been named to the top educational positions in HEW. But in the previous administration, two former university presidents sat in the cabinet—one as attorney general and one as secretary of HEW—and their impact on the bureaucracy was slight. The truth is that cabinet officers are no longer able to control the bureaucracies that they ostensibly direct. Those bureaucracies are so large, and the laws and regulations they administer so complex that they constitute an independent force in government.

Unlike Gellhorn and Boyer, I do not counsel accommodation to the bureaucracy set loose by a Congress so intent on legislating away every inequity that it scarcely takes time to consider whether the problem is susceptible of legislative solution in the first place. Instead of accommodation, I urge that higher education consider whether it needs the protection of an amendment to the U.S. Constitution establishing the autonomy of educational institutions and their right of self-governance. As Thomas Emerson has noted in his book, *The System of Freedom of Expression*, "The function a university is called upon to perform in our society, as the whole theory of academic freedom stresses, cannot be carried out unless the university remains an autonomous institution, independent of the other institutions of our society that it must criticize."[4]

If the protection by constitutional amendment of the independence of universities from federal intrusion seems radical, note that there already exists a statutory prohibition against federal control of education. Section 432 of the General Education Provisions Act states, in pertinent part,

> No provision of any applicable program shall be construed to authorize any department, agency, officer, or employee of the United States to exercise any direction, supervision, or control over the curriculum, program of instruction, administration, or personnel of any educational institution, school, or school system, or over the selection of library resources, textbooks, or other printed or published instructional materials by any educational institution or school system. . . .

The problem, of course, is that this language, being only statutory, leaves Congress quite free to abrogate its terms by subsequent legislative acts, either directly or indirectly. Moreover, the executive branch of government has paid this statute no deference at all; some bureaucrats within HEW have even declared it a nullity without benefit of repeal by Congress or a declaration of unconstitutionality by a court of competent jurisdiction. Therefore, the time may have arrived when the idea expressed in the statute warrants elevation to the level of constitutional protection.

In the end, one's view as to whether the new federal presence on campus is desirable, and to what degree it should be tolerated, depends on the value attached to academic self-determination and independence from government control. I believe that government control and academic freedom are largely incompatible, that there is a natural tendency of government to stifle inquiry, to smother innovation, and to be intolerant of diversity and individualism. If current trends continue unabated, the nation will suffer a homogenization of its colleges and universities. The competitive striving for excellence that has given us universities of distinction will be gone as G.S. 13s and 14s in Washington dictate an abandonment of merit standards and apportion to each institution the students *they* select to be taught a curriculum *they* design by faculty whom *they* deem adequate. I find this prospect intolerable. History has taught us it is a risky business to trust one's welfare to a benevolent government.

NOTES

1. 512 F.2d 556.
2. 538 F.2d 1317; cert. granted, 45 U.S.L.W. 3686.
3. G. LaNoue, "Athletics and Equality: How to Comply with Title IX Without Tearing Down the Stadium," *Change* Magazine 8 (November 1976), p. 64.
4. T. Emerson, *The System of Freedom of Expression* (New York: Random House, 1970), p. 624.

Chapter 5

By Hemp or by Silk, The Outcome is the Same

Robert L. Ketter

Many persons both in and out of government frequently make higher education the same offer that was made to the condemned man who was asked whether he preferred to be hanged with coarse hemp or smooth silk. The most favorable outlook higher education has been presented concerning the future course of government regulation is that it will become less onerous as accommodation and compromise increase between the regulators and regulated. In short, the rope will not scratch, though the outcome will be the same.

It is true that higher education can learn to adjust much better to the regulatory process. However, there are consequences of such an adjustment just as there are consequences of controls per se; and these obtain whether the regulation is imposed by the judicial, the legislative, or the executive branch—or even by a particular institution.

Every university and college is aware that judicial decisions have necessitated more precisely worded standards of employment and conduct, as well as the development of fair-hearing procedures. These unquestionably have altered the informal manner—some would say the capricious and authoritarian manner—in which such matters once were handled. Administratively, the standards and procedures are not difficult to develop; only time and the careful use of language are required. Clearly stated standards are desirable, and the notion of a fair hearing certainly is unobjectionable in academe. In fact, one can argue that higher education has always been more receptive to the concept of fairness, and more conscientious in its application, than virtually any other segment of society. One indication of academe's sensitivity is the fact that so few faculty members are ever dismissed for cause.

Nevertheless, the development of standards and procedures for hearings pertaining to employment and conduct may prevent some administrators from initiating action they otherwise might take. And once a matter goes to hearing, it is questionable whether the elaborately codified standards and procedures produce decisions markedly different from those that would otherwise have been made. Most university and college presidents will not voluntarily relinquish their final administrative authority. Whether in a public or private institution, these presidents are ultimately accountable to other persons, usually a board, whose members likely reflect a range of values and standards acceptable to the community and applicable to the particular institution. If the president values his employment and believes in his task, he is not apt to make judgments that might prove to be grossly offensive or outrageous to those persons to whom he is accountable. The standards he applies, therefore, will probably be the same whether codified or not.

Some presidents, of course, might prefer to relinquish their authority in such matters. However, the board—and even the institution's public—is not apt to permit such avoidance of responsibility. An individual must be available who can be held accountable, and the president ultimately is that person.

Hearings obviously can delay decisions and, as a result, create frustration. Moreover, involved procedures can diminish the likelihood that marginal violations of standards of employment or of conduct will be pursued. The effort required may be too time-consuming and therefore too costly. Finally, inadvertent procedural violations also are possible, in which case a judgment may be voided or reached on procedural grounds alone. At best, such consequences may be tolerated, but never applauded.

Professors Gellhorn and Boyer state that the most important development in due process applied to institutions may be that governing boards and administrators "have not stopped at the edge of minimum legality." To the extent that judicially established limits are being exceeded, it is possible that higher education is exacerbating all of the consequences previously noted. Due process is not only begetting additional procedures, it is begetting them in areas that the courts have not yet touched. For instance, in substantive academic decisions, the University at Buffalo has instituted both undergraduate and graduate student procedures through which students may challenge the determinations of faculty, even in matters of grades. Although the procedural requirements in such instances may be less time-consuming than those that apply in cases involving student or employee dismissal, nevertheless they do require relatively formal hearings in the presence of all affected parties.

Tenure and promotion procedures are much more elaborate. In this area, as in many others where institutions have established detailed procedural constraints, a crucial question is seldom addressed: Are the procedures really necessary? Yet it is this same question that higher education accuses regulatory agencies of avoiding. Institutions may too frequently impose overly detailed structures upon the entire institution in order to guard against disruptive but rare exceptions.

Another significant factor in the establishment of hearing procedures has been the advent of unions. Institutions must be exceedingly careful in their treatment of provisions included within agreements concerning conditions of employment. It is in litigation in these areas that courts are tempted to intrude directly into substantive issues requiring the exercise of academic judgment. Even decisions concerned only with questions of procedure can have substantive import when action is overturned on the basis of a procedural violation of the contract.

Many have begun to criticize the imposition of legalistic models upon higher education, a criticism that is not merely a reflection of aggravation or of an inability to adjust to changing circumstances. Its roots lie much deeper and it is not unjustified, despite higher education's otherwise basic respect for clearly defined standards and fair hearings.

Higher education has been grounded administratively in the processes of consultation and collegiality. At most institutions, at least, such has been the ideal. In these processes authority may be exercised, but seldom power. The concept of power, in fact, is alien to the participants. However, the introduction of a plethora of formalized procedures for decisions and grievances of all types has slowly eroded reliance on informal consultation and collegiality. Recent attitudes reflect the opinion that consultation with a particular person or group is not a significant responsibility to meet if it is not specifically required by institutional procedures or the labor contract. Procedures become more important than the quality of human relationships, and an informal collegial society gradually becomes rigidly codified in its processes. Moreover, to the extent that institutional procedures are patterned after trial procedures, the campus becomes a place in which relationships among various persons and constituencies are adversarial. In such circumstances, power can indeed come into play. The imposition of legalistic models, therefore, can clearly affect the quality of human relationships with academe, and one result may be the slow demise of collegiality.

Relationships may also be affected by legal requirements that official meetings and records be open to the public. Of course, one might be cynical and suggest that such statutes and judicial decisions will make no substantial difference in the business that is conducted; only the procedures for conducting it will change. More decisions will be decided unofficially before being unveiled officially. At most, decision-making may become more cumbersome without becoming more enlightened.

In discussing faculty promotion and tenure procedures, however, Professors Gellhorn and Boyer suggest "the need for candor and the necessity for maintaining an ongoing relationship with the candidate," and they express a sensitivity to the proper maintenance of human relationships. Unfortunately, the "open-meeting" statutes do not embody these concerns. If business is truly conducted openly, necessary ongoing relationships are likely to be damaged through candid discussions which become unduly publicized and in which no face-saving devices for participants are readily available. Neither administrative discretion nor participant restraint will preclude the outcome. Yet efforts at prevention probably will be made, and the result will be that the administrator, his advisors, and those to whom he is accountable, may become tainted by an alleged conspiracy to avoid the requirement that the meetings be open. One wonders whether the open-meeting statutes were the result of a genuine public demand to know, or were simply in response to various special-interest groups. If the latter, then the openness they require may well serve an adversial, undesirable purpose within higher education.

The most onerous aspect of regulation, many educators suggest, is that which emanates from the regulatory bureaucracies themselves, abetted by the judicial and legislative branches of government. Such regulation has been criticized as costly and often duplicative, as unnecessarily intrusive in its concerns, and as burdensome in its reporting requirements. The regulations themselves are frequently paraded as prime examples of obtuseness, and the regulators as ignorant of what they are regulating. On the other hand, agency and congressional critics have complained about the inability of higher education to present a united front when matters crucial to education have been at issue. They have criticized the overabundance of rhetoric and the underabundance of fact with which higher education has attempted to explain itself. And they have taken delight at the irony of liberal educators complaining about regulation.

Government regulation is indeed costly for both higher education and society. A study published last year by the American Council on Education revealed that total costs for twelve federally mandated social programs at only six public and private institutions had increased during the decade 1965–1975 from a combined $500,000 to $10 million. Administrative costs of the programs increased from the miniscule to as much as one-eighth and even one-fourth of total general administrative expense. *Nation's Business* states that the burden of such paperwork costs business $40 billion annually; and *U.S. News and World Report* cites an estimate that 75,000 government employees are now engaged in regulatory activity.

One asks what is obtained by these staggering expenditures of resources. Increased costs for goods and services, including tuition, is one result. Institutions are subjected to duplicative (and sometimes contradictory) requirements by regulations that reportedly fill 60,000 pages of the *Federal Register* annually with small print. A Circular Letter of the National Association of State Universities and Land-Grant Colleges reported some months ago that proposed regulations for the protection of human subjects had been issued separately by the Energy Research and Development Administration, by the Consumer Product Safety Commission, and by the Food and Drug Administration. Department of Health, Education, and Welfare regulations in this area already existed.

Such expenditures certainly have not contributed to the advancement of the English language. This is an old complaint, reaching back at least to Franklin Roosevelt, who reduced federal blackout instructions to one succinct and direct sentence. "Turn out the lights or cover the windows." Of course, obtuse regulations provide more opportunities for regulators to issue interpretations or clarifying memoranda; and in this manner, the bureaucracy is able to keep itself busy.

Professors Gellhorn and Boyer characterize higher education's reaction to government regulation as overreaction—as if regulation "were as dangerous as the McCarthyism of the fifties." Frankly, any central government that can regulate the sexual composition of grammar school choirs can aspire to regulate everything. The tendency is dangerous and should not be minimized. Regulation has intruded directly or indirectly into such substantive areas as hiring, admission, curriculum, as well as into resource allocation.

Charles B. Saunders, Jr. suggested recently in the *Educational Record* that it will do no good simply to rail at regulation; instead, higher education must learn to educate its regulators and to function effectively within the bureaucratic process. The start is already underway. A group of educators provided recommendations for the government's Interagency Task Force on Higher Education Burden Reduction. Greater efforts are being made by the various educational associations toward "consciousness-raising" among lawmakers and regulators. Also, as Professors Gellhorn and Boyer have intimated, higher education must become—and, in fact, is becoming—less reluctant to challenge the regulatory agencies in the courts; in other words, it must take the adversarial relationship to its ultimate conclusion.

We are told, too, that the government will soon require the regulators to learn the English language, to take credit for their creations, to question the need for particular regulations, to determine whether data requirements are necessary—in sum, to be aware of the overall impact of regulation. Perhaps all this shall come to pass; on the other hand, perhaps then we shall have only more comfortable regulation in increasing amounts.

Such efforts involve no more than changing the quality of the rope with which one is to be hanged. The problem is more basic. Derek Bok alluded to it when he spoke of Harvard's independence and freedom. Former Secretary of Health, Education and Welfare, David Mathews, mentioned it when he noted that the public reaction to "bizarre examples of 'governmentese' " was no longer humorous but resented. Each observation points unerringly to the realization that government, in the pursuit of what it terms public policy, has only succeeded in alienating the public. Indeed, consciously or unconsciously, government has created an adversarial relationship between large segments of the public and itself, just as we have seen such relationships develop within higher education.

If relationships among persons, institutions and government have been damaged and not merely changed by the great preoccupation with procedural and regulatory requirements, then the question is whether and how the damage can be repaired. Robert Andringa, minority staff director of the Committee on Education and Labor in the House of Representatives, has suggested that the glut of government lawyers be put to work writing and rewriting laws and regulations so that more good faith is presumed—so that innocence rather than culpability is the first assumption. Instead of centralizing authority and functions, the law should emphasize personal, institutional, and governmental autonomy, as well as interdependence. Such a redirection might serve the restoration of the sense of community that seems to have been so badly eroded in this nation. It can not occur, of course, without trust— trust among persons, institutions, and governments in the judgments and food faith efforts of one another. This is the end that regulation could and should serve. I hope we have not passed the point of such trust, for the alternative is that persons and institutions increasingly pit themselves as adversaries against a government that purports to serve them.

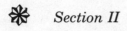 *Section II*

Government Regulation and the Academic Occupation

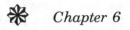 *Chapter 6*

The Impact of Government Regulation on the Academic Occupation

Alfred D. Sumberg

In this chapter we shall analyze not simply the problems presented to academe by the fact of government regulation, but more generally those related issues that together describe the changing relationship between government and the community of scholars.[a]

We begin with a historical perspective. Major social, economic, and political changes that have influenced our society since the 1950s have had a direct impact upon higher education. Over the past two decades the nation has undergone (a) the most recent of several social revolutions, (b) the reversal of a long-term pattern of economic growth, and (c) a disturbance in the stability of its political institutions.

The social revolution was formally inaugurated in 1954 by the decision of the U.S. Supreme Court in *Brown v. Board of Education*, which established the right of minorities to participation in the mainstream of American education. For higher education, the subsequent efforts by successive presidents, courts, and Congress to remove the obstacles to such participation that confront Blacks and other minorities, and by the civil rights movement to encourage the utilization of newly created opportunities, have been dramatic in their impact. While courts and presidents attacked discriminatory admissions policies, Congress provided funds to students and institutions in order

[a] The interpretations and conclusion are those of the author and do not necessarily reflect the formal views of the American Association of University Professors.

to accelerate the transition. In the context of civil rights legislation, Congress passed the Higher Education Act of 1965 and later the Education Amendments of 1972. Both were designed to increase access to higher education for the new group of minority and disadvantaged students by offering a variety of financial assistance programs. The result was an immediate and sharp increase in enrollments primarily at public colleges and universities but also at private institutions. The by-product of this new pattern in student enrollments was, of course, a change in academic employment policies designed to increase the numbers and percentages of Blacks and other minorities on faculties and administrative staffs.

As part of the general social revolution, the women's rights movement also directed its attention to faculty and administration employment practices, particularly to discrimination against women in matters of hiring, promotion, tenure, and compensation. Consistent with the practices of earlier women's rights efforts, the current movement looked first to Congress and then to the courts for the legal validation of their claims. However, initial successes there (for example, disposing earlier antinepotism regulations) gave way to much slower progress in other areas, including promotions, tenure, compensation, retirement benefits, grievance procedures, and access to fellowships and grants.[1]

The economic decline brought directly to the campus the twin evils of unemployment and inflation. Paradoxically, while the high rate of unemployment severely diminished the opportunities available to graduates entering the labor market, it also brought unemployed students to the campus, forced others to change career goals, and required of increasing numbers that they become part-time students. The impact upon faculty employment was severe. There are fewer full-time faculty in four-year institutions in 1977 than there were in 1974. Retrenchment by some institutions brought about faculty dismissals, and even more widespread difficulties were posed by the immobility of faculty and the limited availability of teaching positions for people who recently completed graduate work.

The second evil, inflation, disrupted institutional budgets, led to a gradual increase in tuitions and to a substantial increase in the students' cost of living, and brought a decline in faculty salaries. Erosion of salaries was initially evident in 1968, but academic year 1973–1974 marked the first time since the beginning of AAUPs annual survey that faculty salary and compensation levels fell below the increase in cost of living. The years between 1972 and 1975, moreover, experienced a 10 percent decrease in the real salaries of faculty.[2]

The social revolution and the economic decline forced a reordering of priorities within the academic community. But it was the third factor, the instability of representative government, that had the devastating impact upon the relationships between government and the nation's academics. After the escalation of American involvement in Vietnam in 1966, the campus served over the next several years as the primary forum for protests against the war and against the president responsible for its escalation. The backlash of those protests, aided and abetted by an executive who was blatantly anticampus, was merely a symptom of latent cynicism about the quality of current educational programs and their value to society and to the individual. A revived McCarthyism was visited upon institutions, students, and faculty, and the academic community was no more ready to defend itself against the new attack than it had been ready to do so in the early 1950s. As a consequence, representatives of higher education found it increasingly difficult to present their case for continued high levels of priority and support to Congress, to state legislatures, to corporate and individual contributors, and to the general public. To make matters worse, higher education was caught in the middle of new political struggles over which it had little control, conflicts between Congress and the executive over the impoundment of appropriated funds, over annual budgets for HEW, and over the extension of federal agency jurisdiction to include higher education. As many observers have pointed out, the academic community was not prepared, either psychologically or structurally, for the increased federal role in higher education affairs, nor for the urgent task of developing a coherent strategy to reverse the declining national priority assigned to higher education. Moreover, the federal government manifested so little consistency in its policies and diverse programs affecting higher education that the difficult task confronting academe would have been virtually impossible in any event.

Government and the academic community now face crucial decisions concerning their relationship. The social revolution has not met its minimum goals for the academic employment or admissions of either minorities or women. Indeed, retrogression appears to have occurred, created in part by those economic conditions that slowed the earlier momentum in funding and growth. Even a renewed confidence in government would not presage a sudden resurrection of priority for higher education in national policy.

Several questions arise concerning government: Does government intend to move rapidly, firmly, and without reservation toward removing obstacles to employment and admission faced by minorities and toward eliminating discrimination against women? Does it intend to expand employment opportunities for college graduates? Does it intend to provide the financial assistance necessary to permit institutions to retain current faculty and to help new faculty find positions? Does it intend to relieve the extraordinary burden that inflation has placed on higher education? Does it intend to create a unified and consistent federal policy toward higher education?

For the academic community, the counterpart questions concern primarily higher education's ability to resolve some of these problems by internal action. In particular, will academe move rapidly, firmly, and without reservation toward removing discriminatory obstacles faced by minorities and women? Will it develop a strategy to increase enrollments, expand the number of graduates for a growing labor force, expand the number of full-time faculty, and contain the costs of education in order to maintain low and equitable tuitions?

In the context of the general topic, namely, the character and appropriateness of government regulation of higher education, the foregoing questions yield precedence to the basic inquiry: Is higher education an overregulated industry that ought to be deregulated?[3] No, for two very different reasons. First, compared with other areas of economic activity, higher education is relatively free from the complex regulation of trade and industry that dates back to the 1790s. And second, government regulation of higher education has a social purpose directly related to the basic purpose of the academy—gathering and disseminating knowledge. Government encourages those who are qualified intellectually but who are in need financially to "arm themselves," as James Madison said, "with the power which knowledge gives."

Critics, however, might well suggest three contrary observations. First, there is the danger that despite the silence of the federal Constitution regarding education and the reservation thereby of authority in such matters to the states, the federal government will nonetheless assume control of higher education. In the Higher Education Act of 1965, of course, Congress eschewed federal control over the curriculum, program of instruction, administration, personnel, and selection of library resources of any educational institution. In addition, the Education Amendments of 1976 extended the prohibition specifically to all programs under the jurisdiction of the Education Division of the Department of Health, Education and Welfare. Yet, to some students of academe, the federal government appears closer today in both the scope and the detail of its activity to a pervasive control of higher education than at any time in our history. Second, we can see a change in the attitudes of academics toward the federal government: "A fundamental change is taking place in the relationship between Washington and the nation's colleges and universities. Once we were partners, working together to solve national problems. Now, we view each other with suspicion—almost as adversaries. If our partnership is to be restored, it urgently needs our attention and understanding."[4] And third, the cost to academe of regulation by Washington is at the bottom of much current disagreement between institutions and the federal government.[5]

Are the policies and behavior of academics closer today to control by the federal government than at any previous time? On the one hand, federal officials protest they do not wish to exercise such control either by legislation or by regulation. On the other hand, an increasing amount of legislation and regulation, both adopted and proposed, moves dangerously into the gray area. At one moment, the issue is accreditation; at the next, the percentage of veterans or other recipients of federal student assistance in the classrooms; and at another, the admissions policies of medical schools. Nevertheless, I submit that "control by the federal government" is too narrow a description of academe's current difficulty to withstand scrutiny. More accurately, the problem is that of a general erosion of institutional autonomy under attack from a variety of parties, including the very states that historically have guaranteed that autonomy.

The academic community can conceivably affect the substance of federal legislation if it will pay attention to process. The House and Senate authorizing subcommittees which have jurisdiction over higher education legislation are accustomed to holding extensive hearings and encouraging a broad cross section of the academic community to participate. Legislation does not necessarily result directly from the hearings but it is helpful in placing the issues in perspective. More importantly, as Robert Andringa, the astute director of minority staff for the House Education and Labor Committee points out, the primary force in shaping federal education laws is the personal judgment and values of usually not more than six to ten members of Congress and their assistants.[6] The substance of legislation frequently reflects a series of current or projected programs that members of the respective subcommittees, aided and abetted by their staffs, lobbyists, and perhaps the administration, believe should be funded.[7] In short, the presentation in hearings of relevant position papers on specific programs, and discussion with members of the subcommittees and their staff, provide the outlines of specific provisions in any legislation currently under consideration.

In any discussion of the "adversarial" relationship between academe and the federal government, and of the cost to academe of government regulation, one does well to pay special attention to the Education Amendments of 1976. The 1976 amendments demonstrated Congress' continuing support of improving student access (1) by increasing the maximum Basic Educational Opportunity Grant from $1400 to $1800, (2) by expanding the special programs for students from disadvantaged backgrounds, (3) by establishing educational information centers, (4) by requiring the dissemination of substantial information about financial assistance, costs of attendance, refund policies, and academic programs to both current and prospective students, (5) and by establishing graduate programs for minority groups traditionally underrepresented in higher education. But the Education Amendments of 1976 were also concerned, however minimally, with the quality of education. They provided support for research libraries, graduate education, innovative programs, and the new lifelong learning program. For the concerned campus administrator, there was provision for administrative cost allowances, for the training of student financial aid officers, and for support of reconstruction and reconversion of campus facilities to meet new energy requirements, new standards of health and safety, environmental protection, and access for the handicapped. Finally, in recognition of the outcries over burdensome paperwork, Section 406 attempted to reduce the amount of paperwork and to eliminate duplication in the collection of information and data.

The Education Amendments of 1976 included both new authorizations and extensions of older authorizations. Funding of some of the authorized programs will occur in the FY 1977 Supplemental Appropriations Bill and the FY 1978 Budget, although the bulk of the new authorizations will not be funded until President Carter drafts his budget for FY 1979. Some of the authorizations, of course, will never be funded. Of immediate interest, however, are the regulations drafted by the United States Office of Education for the administration of the funded programs. The Office of Education estimates that it will take about three dozen sets of regulations to interpret and implement the funded programs under the education amendments. Eight of those proposed regulations have already been published; four were published in the Federal Register of April 8. There will be public hearings at various locations around the country, and there will be ample opportunity to comment on the proposed regulations in detail either at the hearings or in writing. Those proposed regulations require careful reading at the campus level and should be read in the context of experiences with those programs on the campus. Both written comments and oral testimony are carefully considered by the appropriate officials of the Office of Education and frequently revision is necessary prior to the issuance of final regulations. If past practice is followed, however, there will be only a handful of comments and little testimony submitted. Then at some later day, faculty and campus administrators will find themselves in conflict with some provision of the final regulations and they will wonder openly and articulately about how the regulations were drafted.

The transition from legislation to regulations comes very quickly, at least in the minds of Washington observers. It is standard procedure among pundits to cite the extraordinary growth in the number of regulations issued by executive agencies and independent commissions since the 1930s and to use this evidence, as indicated by the bulky pages of the daily *Federal Register*, to criticize the regulatory process. In a recent report on CBS News, Roger Mudd pointed out that the agencies that churn out the most regulations are the Departments of Agriculture, Health, Education and Welfare, Transportation, and the Internal Revenue Service.[8] The drafting process per se within the Office of Education and HEW is a complete mystery to most casual observers. Under former HEW secretary, Caspar Weinberger, the process was one of absolute secrecy and no discussion prior to the issuance of draft regulations between regulators and the regulated was permitted. Discussion took place only after the proposed regulations were published in the *Federal Register*. Secretary Mathews, however, reversed that policy in a memorandum of July 25, 1976, in which he provided for public participation prior to the drafting of the proposed regulations.[9] And Secretary Califano has moved to obtain more effective public participation in HEWs day-to-day operations, including the regulatory process.[10]

We should understand that not all legislation requires the subsequent issuance of regulations. At the same time, however, it is a wise and honored practice for Congress not to include the minute details of administration of every authorized program in legislation. Therefore, when reading proposed regulations, one should analyze carefully the legislation and its legislative history, including committee reports and the debates on the floors of the House and Senate. The purpose of analyzing proposed regulations is to understand what it is that Congress intended and how the executive agency interprets that intent. Perhaps the most controversial aspect of regulations is found in the attempt of regulation writers to interpret congressional silence. Just how does one interpret the intent underlying a program when one finds only a statutory provision bare of any reference thereto in the committee reports and of any discussion during the course of floor action? The common outcome is that members of Congress and interested parties outside of Congress charge that agencies attempt to write law through regulations, as witness the controversies over Title IX regulations and the regulations for the Buckley Amendment.

Despite such difficulties, however, when we listen carefully to the outcries against the federal regulatory process, we find only a handful of people who absolutely condemn regulation in principle. In a recent article entitled "Is Federal Regulation a Threat to Academic Freedom?" President McGill of Columbia University, which in 1975 ranked seventh in the nation in the dollar amount of federal support given such institutions, recited all of the usual horror stories about regulations, and made several useful recommendations for revision of the regulatory process. But then he answered the title question by asserting that regulation is not a threat to academic freedom in principle, only that "we appear to be moving in worrisome directions." In his article, President McGill reflects a sensitivity to the abuses that legislation and regulations attempt to eliminate. Yet his argument, in the final analysis, is not with the principle of federal regulation but with the regulators.[11]

Within recent years, others have expressed similar doubts ranging from concern over the inadequate data available to regulation writers in HEW to the impact on academic self-governance of both regulations and the administration of federal monies. There are, however, efforts at reform underway. In his fireside chat of February 2, President Carter said: "We'll cut down also on government regulations, and we'll make sure that those that are written are in plain English for a change. Whenever a regulation is issued, it will carry its author's name. And I will request the Cabinet members to read all regulations personally before they are released."[12] Obviously, such a declaration in and of itself does not resolve the problems inherent in the regulatory process, but it is an important beginning—and the responsibility for monitoring carefully the regulatory process as well as the substance of government regulation rests heavily upon the academic community. In addition, there is currently a genuine effort underway, in the federal government generally and in HEW specifically, to reduce the burden of paperwork. Finally, reform through reorganization has been undertaken both by Secretary Califano and Commissioner of Education Ernest Boyer, although the necessary reform, namely, the creation of a separate Department of Education, is still in the future.

The role of the states in the regulation of higher education is a subject that needs more careful analysis today than ever before. The most informative commentary I know on the current relationships between the states and higher education, published in 1976 by the Carnegie Foundation for the Advancement of Teaching,[13] confirms what knowledgeable persons in government relations have been saying for several years: Many of the problems institutions face with the federal government exist also at the state level—intrusion on governance, imposition of paperwork, and diversion of scarce resources to useless bureaucratic activity.

The basic issue that higher education confronts in its current relationship with government is how it can most productively contribute to resolving the problems of a society that is attempting to fulfill its democratic goals. If one accepts the premise that democracy and education are inextricably linked, then the political and social institutions that foster those goals have extraordinary, perhaps unique, responsibilities to one another. First, the academic community must improve student access and the quality of education, and it must eliminate discrimination in its personnel practices. Federal authorities, in turn, must provide leadership among the several levels of government, and must adequately fund both students and institutions. Of the two, the burden, in my judgment, falls more heavily on the academic community. After two decades of gradual change, it now has the opportunity to seize the initiative and to meet internally those goals of the social revolution that apply to higher education. It would be a serious miscalculation for the academic community to remain passive, for though it is hardly feasible that the federal government resolve such problems alone, the government is capable of exerting sufficient pressure to force hasty, ill-conceived action by the academic community itself.

Second, there needs to be a searching and thoughtful campus dialogue not only on the immediate difficulties of government regulation but also on the larger issues of higher education's proper role in its environment. What are the responsibilities of the academic community to a democratic society in transition? What is happening to academic governance and institutional autonomy? What is the impact of higher education on the community, state, nation, and world? What is the appropriate relationship between government and faculty in the areas of teaching and research? As Alan Pifer, president of the Carnegie Corporation, pointed out in his 1975 report:

"The building of a new consensus about the place of higher education in our national life, and reversal of the present negativism toward it, is an enormous task, involving public officials, leading citizens, young people, the general public and, most of all, academic institutions themselves. No one can promise that this urgent undertaking will succeed. If it does not, however, it will not be higher education alone but the entire nation that will be at risk, for what is at stake is no less than this." [14]

Third, I believe we need to be more realistic about the current nature of the academic marketplace. Walter Adams of Michigan State University has described it in terms that need to be understood throughout the academic community:

On various occasions I have tried to make this point to leaders in education and government. I have tried to explain that the academic marketplace is not an autonomous or divine mechanism; that the demand for higher education is not natural, but artificial; that it is not conditioned by exogenous forces, but determined by man-made decisions of federal, state, and local governments; that such decisions need not, as a matter of logic, favor guns over education; in short, that a reorientation of our national priorities to reflect more accurately the needs of the people, and to deal more effectively with the challenge of our times, would very quickly transmute higher education from a depressed into a thriving industry, operating at overfull capacity and beset by chronic shortages of badly needed talent.[15]

If Adams is correct, and I believe he is, then the academic community bears the responsibility for making the strong case for that position to the leaders of the federal, state, and local governments. Such efforts will obviously require the strengthening of institutional government relations programs and the increased utilization of faculty, administrative, trustee, and student representatives in such programs.

Last, while the regulation issue bears close analysis and critique, it also requires that the academic community become throughly involved in the process by which legislation and regulations are drafted. When legislation is approved, it becomes incumbent upon the chief administrator of each individual campus to determine how the legislation in question may affect the programs on that campus and to communicate that information to the appropriate federal officials, including the regulation writers. At every step in the regulation process, campus involvement is essential if the regulations are to enhance rather than obstruct the implementation of legitimate federal action.

NOTES

1. "Report of Committee W, 1975–76," *AAUP Bulletin* 62 (August 1976): 192–94.

2. "Nearly Keeping Up: Report on the Economic Status of the Profession, 1975–76," ibid., 195–207.

3. Government regulation is here defined broadly to include legislation, executive agency rules and regulations, and judicial review. Emphasis is upon the federal government.

4. Quoted in Louis W. Bender, *Federal Regulation and Higher Education* (Washington, D.C.: American Association for Higher Education, 1977), p. 16.

5. See Carol Van Alstyne and Sharon L. Coldren. *The Costs of Implementing Federally Mandated Social Programs at Colleges and Universities* (Washington, D.C.: American Council on Education, 1976).

6. Andringa lists the Congressional hearings as number seven on his list of eleven factors significant in shaping legislation.

7. Symposium on "Federalism at the Crossroads: Improving Educational

Policymaking," Institute for Educational Leadership, George Washington University, Washington, D.C., 1976.

8. Transcript, "CBS Evening News with Walter Cronkite," April 8, 1977.

9. David Mathews, Memorandum, July 25, 1976.

10. Letter from Secretary Joseph A. Califano, Jr., March 28, 1977, enclosing "Summary of the Report of the Task Force on Citizen Participation."

11. William McGill, "Is Federal Regulation a Threat to Academic Freedom?" *Columbia Today* (March 1977) pp. 2, 34–36.

12. Transcript, "Remarks of the President in an Address to the Nation," February 2, 1977.

13. Carnegie Foundation for the Advancement of Teaching, *The States and Higher Education* (New York, 1976).

14. Alan Pifer, *Higher Education in the Nation's Consciousness* (New York: Carnegie Corp., 1975).

15. Walter Adams, "The State of Higher Education: Myths and Realities," *AAUP Bulletin* 60 (Summer 1974): 121. See also Walter Adams, "Financing Public Higher Education," *American Economic Review* (February 1977), pp. 86–89.

Chapter 7

Government Regulation, Institutional Self-Regulation, and Access to Academic Employment

Sheila Tobias

Affirmative action and special minority admissions programs are being threatened. The *Bakke* case, which will be heard by the U.S. Supreme Court in October, and the recent attempt by the Congress to prohibit HEW from imposing "ratios, quotas, timetables . . ." on federally funded programs puts those of us who advocate change in the race and sex profile of college faculty and students again on the defensive. As far as government regulation of the "academic occupation" is concerned, the issue is quite simply: (1) whether there is something particularly inappropriate about affirmative action (especially the use of goals and timetables) as a system for remedying past discrimination when required of colleges and universities; and (2) whether in the absence of government regulation colleges and universities could and would effectively monitor themselves to increase access by women and minorities to employment and to provide more socially responsible employment practices generally.

INTRODUCTION

It has been alleged that the cost of government regulation of colleges and universities both in loss of autonomy and in actual expenditures is not worth whatever benefits derive from such regulation. The academy, it is argued, is a unique employer—self-governing, collegial rather than hierarchic, and dependent upon academic freedom in conducting its business as well as in performing its research. Any upset in the delicate balance represented in traditional university governance may destroy the sanctity, the integrity, and the quality of university life.

Whether or not this is an idealized vision of a small percentage of postsecondary institutions, nonetheless in the context of this model affirmative action requirements have been viewed as more alien and destructive to the academic environment than has any other aspect of government regulation. Apart from the perceived rigidity of goals or "quotas" there is a fundamental difference between recruitment for the construction industry, where affirmative action began, and recruitment for academic teaching and scholarship, where skills are nonstandard and noninterchangeable.[1] Affirmative action is considered by its most severe critics to impose on employers "an inflexible requirement to hire a fixed number or percentage of minorities or women . . . leading inevitably to the hiring of unqualified or less qualified people."[2]

The use of numbers in the form of goals and timetables as a way of enforcing the legal prohibitions against job discrimination was put forward by the National Association for the Advancement of Colored People in the last half of the 1950s as a way for the courts to direct employers to remedy past job inequality. First used in the construction industry but later extended to the white collar workforce, the principle of affirmative action was specified by the courts to mean, for example, that in the case of building contractors, a minimum number of Blacks and other minority workers would be employed in each craft at every stage of construction. This concept was later incorporated within the Philadelphia Plan which, though challenged in the federal courts, was found again and again to be an appropriate remedy. A number of cases, which the Supreme Court declined to review, established the legal validity of the principle of "affirmative relief" in the form of hiring and promotional targets or goals.[3]

Unfortunately, the evolution of this remedy was not widely noted outside the legal and civil rights professions in those years. Few academics commented on the unequivocal argument in support of numeric goals in Charles Silverman's *The Crisis in Black and White*:

> As soon as we agree that special measures are necessary to overcome the heritage of past discrimination, the question of numbers—of how many Negroes are to be hired in what job categories—inevitably arises. Not to use numbers as a yardstick for measuring performance is, in effect, to revert to Tokenism. The point is not whether there is some right number of Negroes to be employed, obviously there is not, but simply that *there is no meaningful measure of change other than numbers* (italics added).[4]

Silverman's remedy was based on a particular analysis of past discrimination. Given the nature of that discrimination, any dependence upon voluntary compliance with fair employment practice laws, that is, upon "passive nondiscrimination," was inadequate. "Discrimination in employment," Herbert Hill reiterated in 1975, "is not the result of random acts of malevolence. It does not usually occur because of individual bigotry, but rather is the consequence of systematic institutionalized patterns that are rooted in the society."[5]

If passive nondiscrimination is ineffective against these institutionalized patterns, and if similar patterns exist in colleges and universities, then the issue to be addressed is not whether government regulation is appropriate but rather whether colleges and universities are prepared to undertake the radical action necessary to correct past inequities, with or without government regulation.

THE SPECIAL CASE OF WOMEN IN HIGHER EDUCATION

Many people believe that Executive Order 11246 might never have been applied to colleges and universities had the order not been amended in 1969 to include women. A woman unfairly denied employment at the University of Maryland, and a member of a feminist organization named the Women's Equity Action League, filed a series of claims on behalf of all women against many of the nation's universities. Her action resulted in a ruling by the Office of Federal Contract Compliance in the Department of Labor that colleges and universities that had entered into federal research or building contracts were obliged to prepare and to implement affirmative action plans. Since women are the largest "underutilized" population at the professional level in higher education, a matter to be discussed below, and since affirmative action is designed to achieve a proportional representation of "affected groups," women even more than minorities should have benefited from this decision.

Cynthia Epstein and Helena Astin have each shown in their respective studies of professional women's career patterns that in the past women have been discriminated against at the point of admission-to-training.[6] So long as the pool of women Ph.D.s remained small, the academic employer did not deliberately exclude the woman professional. A large part of that job was being accomplished by what Epstein so aptly calls the gate-keepers, that is, graduate schools, financial aid committees, and even national fellowship programs. Then, in the 1960s, substantial growth occurred in graduate education as part of the wave to catch up with the Soviet's supposed scientific advantage, and women were suddenly welcome to compete for NDEA grants, foundation fellowships, and university stipends. As they did, the number of women doctorates trebled. By 1968, approximately 11 percent of the doctorates in the United States were held by women, 38 percent in French and English literature, 18 percent in biology and sociology, 7 percent in economics, and a low of less than 2 percent in physics. Moreover, many of those doctorates had been earned in very prestigious institutions.

Such rapid growth in the numbers of women Ph.D.s may have caused a shift in the frontier of discrimination. At least so it was perceived by the women coming into professional life in the late 1960s and the early 1970s. The obstacles to professional employment seemed to expand from graduate school admissions to the hiring practices of university faculty. Under these circumstances, an affirmative action strategy having as its target inequities in hiring and promotion could, if enforced, significantly correct the unequal status of women in higher education.

At the same time, during the 1960s universities and colleges found themselves in a new and closer relationship with the federal government. Many universities previously independent of government support entered for the first time into contractual arrangements with federal agencies to do research. Since the bulk of the new money went for scientific research, nonscience departments within the university became relatively poorer by contrast and, consequently, resentful of or even hostile to the new sources of support. It is no accident that resistance to affirmative action and all modes of government regulation of higher education has come nationwide from members of those departments in particular that have benefited little from external funding during the boom period, and have been losing power and prestige internally as well.

Thus, there is a mixture of motives underlying the opposition to affirmative action from the university "vulgarized" by the hiring of women and minority members under the "affirmative action gun" as they put it. They consider federal support itself vulgar, and they resent the shifts in internal institutional power that federal support has produced. They may also resent the fact that a number of issues embedded in the typical university hiring system have been exposed by affirmative action.

TRADITIONAL HIRING PRACTICES

Critics of affirmative action speak of the loss of university autonomy to government interference. What is threatened far more by affirmative action, however, is departmental autonomy and some very old and cherished habits:

1. A hiring system rarely open to the scrutiny of persons outside the given department, and to no one outside the university. Promises of jobs were (and still are) made before jobs were officially announced. Senior professors could and did guarantee jobs to their colleagues' proteges as a quid pro quo. University surveillance over promotion and tenure, though usually built into the procedural requirements, would vary in intensity from department to department, depending upon the power relations enjoyed by the department chairman within the university.
2. Reluctance on the part of many faculty to consider the possibility that their standards of "excellence" might be arbitrary or ideologically biased. Even when a qualified candidate is brought to the campus, it is possible that sincere and honest faculty in the department will not recognize that candidate's ability because she is wearing a skirt, or has a higher pitched voice, a southern style of speaking, or is engaged in research not traditionally valued in the field.
3. A reluctance to recruit from any but a particular group of graduate institutions without consideration of the regional or financial constraints that would discourage minorities and women even from applying to such institutions.

Government regulation is blamed for interfering in these cherished modes of conducting university business. But even had there been no pressure from government to regularize and standardize university hiring, such practices would in any case soon have come to an end. Demands for accountability to a variety of publics, creation of multicampus centralized administrations, and unionization all were undermining these traditions. The hue and cry against government regulation of the academic occupation, then, may at the least be partially misplaced.

BREAKING THE CYCLE—A CASE IN POINT

Wesleyan University employed six women and two Blacks at the professional level in 1967, and today has eighty-eight women and eighteen minorities in those positions. The change took place during a period of no-growth, of even modest decline in some areas. Though the institution was not legally vulnerable to affirmative action requirements, having no federal contracts at the time, it achieved what it did by support from the top. In 1970, a high-level advocate was hired with explicit instruction from the president and the board to modify the recruitment and selection process. As a result of these efforts, a critical mass of minority and female personnel is now in place.

The university has every reason to believe that this critical mass will monitor the institution from within. As members of university committees, they will vote on and implement policy. As members of search committees, they will actively participate in all hiring. As members of the university community they will be informed about and react to what goes on even in areas where they are not personally involved. Eventually, as they become senior faculty and staff, chairpersons of departments, and heads of committees, they will see to it that past discrimination continues to be remedied and that new forms of inequity, however subtle, are not introduced. Wesleyan University, then, after approximately seven years of activity, no longer requires federal regulation, or advocacy, or change agents, or sanctions, or even special attention to the needs of minority and women employees. It is willing to regulate itself and, more importantly, it is able to do so.

Of course if, in the short run, proportional representation is a measure of equity, then clearly the smaller college that is doing some continuous hiring has an easier task redressing inequity than does the large university. In a department of eight faculty, for example, all white and male, where the proportion of women in the national pool is 20 percent and of nonwhites 5 percent, proportional representation can be achieved by hiring one woman in the near future. In a large state university, however, with seventy members in the counterpart department, the next fourteen appointments must go to women to achieve the same 20 percent—but those fourteen appointments may represent 100 percent of all hiring in the next five years. Thus, what might in a small university appear to be a modest goal will seem huge to the larger state school that has no reason to expect fourteen openings.

The large university can, however, initiate other constructive methods of increasing the participation of Blacks and women on its campus. For example, regularizing part-time faculty by providing them with pro-rated benefits, committee responsibilities, and advisees and departmental voting privileges might be an affirmative action worth taking. Or sharing faculty among a consortium may be another way to increase the availability of nonwhites. Whatever the particular limitations, however, a critical mass must be developed if change is to be internalized.

There is little information about the results of voluntary or involuntary affirmative action. Few case studies have been reported and, apart from aggregate statistical surveys of the numbers of women and minorities on faculties (which show little improvement), there are no data that indicate, for example, in which institutions and for what reasons women and minorities have improved their status. We hear about the problems, false searches, "reverse discrimination," and the "revolving door" for young assistant professors who are not being renewed or tenured. But the details of even the small amount of affirmative action that has taken place are yet to be reported in a form that would answer the questions: Has affirmative action worked to benefit women and minorities and, if so, where and under what conditions? Has it benefited or actually harmed the institution? Has it benefited the nation as a whole?

How can cost to the university, assuming there are such cost factors, be accurately assessed if we do not have any record of the benefits? At Wesleyan University there has been no noticeable loss in university autonomy, though there has been considerable intervention in departmental autonomy. Similarly, there has been little increase in the cost of record-keeping, though there have been some incremental expenditures for candidate travel and advertisements. As for loss of quality, no one on the faculty would think so. To the contrary, we are now able to attract women and minority candidates who are much sought after because there is now a community in which they can be made to feel at home. If government had defined affirmative action initially to be no more and no less than a policy of transition to bring institutions to the point where they would successfully regulate themselves, some of the current objections (though by no means all of them) might have been met.

The numerical projections made by the University of California at Berkeley—extrapolating Berkeley's goals to the year 2000—would have been seen as irrelevant and absurd. Complaints about the unworkability of long-term sanctions and about the costs of allegedly limitless reporting to the federal government would also have been better answered. The issue of preference (see below) would likely have remained controversial, but if the phrase "short-term infusion" had been substituted for affirmative action, and had "projections" or "possibilities" been chosen instead of "quotas" or goals, academicians might have better appreciated and better understood a set of regulations designed explicitly to produce a critical mass of women and minorities in higher education.

GOALS AND PREFERENCE

Affirmative action policy was predicated, rightly or wrongly, on the assumption that it would be less burdensome to an institution to be judged on the basis of its numerical success than to be required to delineate in detail the process by which that outcome was to be achieved. This numerical goals orientation, though useful, had an unfortunate fatal flaw, particularly at the level of public acceptance.

For reasons we do not entirely understand, particularized goals were from the beginning considered tantamount to numerical quotas.

Outcome measures of progress toward goals can, at a minimum, raise consciousness. But we would be naive if we did not acknowledge that criticism of affirmative action (begun in 1971 by Sidney Hook of Columbia and Paul Seabury of Berkeley) has today mushroomed into what some people are calling a university cartel against it. The public is beginning to view quotas, like busing, as simply too gross an intervention to be justified even on the basis of righting civil wrongs. Recent developments in the Congress are adding to the momentum of those who oppose goals and timetables. In June, both the House and Senate heard amendments to the health, education and welfare appropriations bill that would have prohibited the federal government from imposing any ". . . timetable, goal, ratio, quota, or other numerical requirement related to race, creed, color, national origin, or sex." The House amendment passed, the Senate version was defeated and the difference is presently being ironed out in conference; but there is strong likelihood that affirmative action as we know it will one day be prohibited by the Congress.

At least as unpopular as numerical goals has been the matter of preference, "the affirmative action override" as it is called at AT&T. To many persons, it is one thing to expand recruitment pools, and to compare the percentages of minorities and women at a given institution with their percentages in the pool. But it is quite another course to select a candidate (who would not ordinarily be selected) because of his or her minority status or gender. This seems not only grossly unfair to the individual who is rejected (constituting "reverse discrimination"); it is also likely to lower the quality of the faculty if practiced repeatedly over time, and it is dangerous in the precedent it establishes for other capricious interference with the merit system. There need be little doubt that during the past several years some misguided college presidents have told their deans to find a woman or a black at any price for the sake of meeting their goals; or a low-prestige department may have found that a woman or a Black was foisted on it to protect a high-prestige department against the necessity of meeting a target. Yet, there probably has been far less reverse discrimination than has been suggested. It is in the very nature of prejudice to assume that no woman or minority person could have won the position on merit alone.

Even were it not otherwise necessary, the issue of preference must be addressed by those who wish to take voluntary action. A book in progress by Jack Greenberg of the NAACP Legal Defense Fund examines past practices of preferences in American legal history to make a stronger case for preference. Greenberg argues that one set of values—affirmative relief—must be balanced against another set of values—individual right to a job—and that historically the choice has always been made in terms of the public good. Such logic supported job preference to veterans, for example. But preference is not always popular, and the issue may eventually be fought out in the Congress where popularity more than logic will prevail.

The fundamental problem with preference is not simply the possibility of reverse discrimination but the all-too-broad definition of the "affected groups." The protected classes, race, and sex may not be appropriate categories for affirmative relief after all. This was Justice Douglas' point in his dissent to *De Funis*, and it is the basis of an American Jewish Committee brief in *Bakke* litigation. The argument is further reinforced by the fact that not all minorities and women are currently experiencing discrimination at all levels of education. If the category were to be "the disadvantaged" rather than "minority" or "female," then affirmative relief and special admissions programs might be provided only to those who need them.[7]

VOLUNTARY SELF-REGULATION: CAN IT WORK?

When members of the academic community speak of voluntary compliance in place of government-regulated affirmative action typically what they mean is that they wish to eliminate not only government interference but numeric goals and timetables as well. If such action, however, is not to become "passive nondiscrimination," additional university activity may yet have to be compromised.

Staffing Plan

Few departments have staffing plans. Only when universities move into long-range fiscal planning do they begin to consider staffing needs in any terms except their immediate interests. But without a staffing plan or at the very least the discussion of long-term staffing expectations, it is difficult to believe that women and minorities will be hired when available or deliberately recruited.

Several institutions have now included long-term staffing considerations in their affirmative action plans. Amherst College has developed a staffing plan that allows for expansion in departments where women and minorities are most likely to be well represented in the pool. Princeton University has devised a "tenure flow" plan to allow for the continued promotion into the tenure ranks of recently hired faculty despite overall retrenchment. Many other universities have acted to correct salary inequities and to improve recruitment; but unless there is a concern for finding positions for minorities and women, "recruitment" (identification) will be ineffective.

Impact Analysis of Administrative and Educational Decisions

Every administrative and most educational decisions can have an impact on the likelihood of attracting and retaining women and minority faculty and administrative staff. To insure that that impact is not negative, or that the negative impact is well understood, every retrenchment plan, curriculum modification, proposed new department or program, or proposed elimination of a program should be weighed against its effect on the minority and female faculty (or students).

Evaluation of Procedures and Practices

Since they affect minority and female personnel, tuition rebate policies, opportunities for internal advancement of staff, benefit packages, provision for part-time employment with pro-rated benefits, provision for part-time tenure, and the like require evaluation.

Visibility on Campus

Women and minorities on campus need ample opportunity to become more visible, more credible, and more powerful.

On a wider level, voluntary compliance should include:

Imaginative Cooperation

Universities can work imaginatively with the federal government, with private foundations, and with the major research institutions on programs that will result in an increase in the pool of women and minorities especially in fields where they have been particularly underrepresented (science and technology, economics, management and dentistry, for example).

Finding Ways to Share Minority and Women Faculty

Where the particular institution cannot attract them on a permanent basis, joint appointments, allowing for one semester at a home campus and one away, can be attractive and gratifying to the individual.

Sharing Information

Plans and practices that work can be shared with administrators of other institutions.

Use of Collective Bargaining

Universities can press for collective bargaining agreements that incorporate sound affirmative action and equal opportunity goals.

Voluntary affirmative action is likely to succeed only if most of the following conditions obtain: a critical mass of women and minorities already in place; strong support from the president and the board of trustees; an advocate-strategist at or near the top of central administration; and outside pressure from advocacy groups, alumni, students, and other local interests. When and if such conditions are realized, then goals, quotas, targets, and timetables may not be necessary; and preferential hiring, as in the experience of Wesleyan University, may be unnecessary.

Massive remedial efforts, in turn, can be reserved for institutions where discrimination is well documented and where there is a demonstrated reluctance on the part of the institutions' managers to change. The courts have always taken the position that extraordinary measures can be imposed to remedy extraordinary problems. No one in 1977 can seriously dispute that despite some progress in a few colleges and universities across the country there is still an extraordinary underutilization of minorities and women in higher education.

REFERENCES

1. R. Lester, *Antibias Regulations of Universities: Faculty Problems and Their Solutions* (New York: McGraw-Hill, 1974). See also review of the book by Sheila Tobias in *Change Magazine*, November 1974.

2. S. Pottinger, address before the Annual Convention of the American Bar Association, 1975.

3. H. Hill, "Affirmative Action and the Quest for Job Equality," paper presented at the Tenth Anniversary of the Equal Employment Opportunities Commission, held at Rutgers University Law School, November 28, 1975.

4. C. Silverman, *Crisis in Black and White* (New York: Random House, 1964).

5. *Op. cit.*

6. C. Epstein, *Women's Place* (Berkeley and Los Angeles: University of California Press, 1970); H. Astin, *The Woman Doctorate in America* (New York: Russell Sage Foundation, 1970).

7. T. V. Purcell, S.J., "Management and Affirmative Action in the Late Seventies," Chapter Three in progress for the Industrial Relations Research Association's 1977 Research Volume, *Equal Rights and Industrial Relations: Framework for Evaluating Institutional Commitment to Minorities,* prepared and published by the ACF. (It is my understanding that a similar guideline for self-evaluation of institutional commitment to women is also being undertaken.)

Chapter 8

Government Regulation and the Staying Power of the Professoriate

Donald H. Wollett

The impact of government regulation on the academic occupation is likely to be minimal. The professoriate seems to have a remarkable capacity to withstand external pressures and to continue, after a few flurries, to function much as it has in the past. Faculties appear to be able to wear out their adversaries by evasion or absorption—an academic adaptation, so to speak, of Muhammad Ali's "ropa-dopa" strategy against George Foreman during the heavyweight title fight in Zaire a few years ago.

It is not clear why faculties have this capacity. Three possibilities come to mind: (1) the mystique of the professoriate that tends to insulate it from crude, sustained political pressures; (2) the ability of the academy to obfuscate decision-making and thus to avoid confrontation;[1] (3) the remarkable staying power of faculty groups.

Recent history supports the thesis. Consider, for instance, the McCarthy Era in the early 1950s with its loyalty oaths and witch hunts. There were serious injustices worked on particular faculty members and, at least in the short run, some adverse impact on academic freedom, even narrowly defined. But this condition passed and made no permanent adverse alteration in anything of significance. Indeed, the McCarthy excesses may have strengthened institutional and political commitments to tenure systems and to freedom of association and expression.

Or consider the late 1960s and early 1970s when there was widespread public disenchantment with universities and colleges caused by antisocial student behavior, coupled with instances of faculty connivance or acquiescence, and aggravated by the general inability of campuses to fashion effective instruments of prevention and control. The problem was worsened by the fact that some faculty members abused the traditions and privileges of the academic occupation in ways that were unacceptable to the public. In the period immediately following the Cambodian incursion, for example, between 22 1/2 and 50 percent of the courses at the University of California at Berkeley were "reconstituted." Professors gave credit to their students, often with As and Bs, without examination, and they terminated conventional educational activity in favor of political protests. Public disenchantment grew into outrage. The California Legislature, in a clear act of reprisal, denied a 5 percent cost-of-living salary increase to only one group of state employees—the faculties of the University of California and what is now the state college and university system. To add to public hostility, the malaise of the economy accentuated taxpayer cost-consciousness, putting at the forefront of political debate the question: Are we getting our money's worth?

There followed a spate of government threats to regulate the academic occupation:

1. Tighter Supervision. One university president urged that deans and department chairpersons take the role of shop supervisors and plant superintendents with supervisory power over courses, curricula, instructional performance, and ratings; authority to assign personnel and to report faculty failures to carry out responsibilities; and power to initiate appropriate corrective action in the event of dereliction or substandard work.
2. Discipline. Another president, in response to threats of government regulation, urged creation of more comprehensive and effective procedures for disciplining members of the faculty. He stated that the faculty could no longer be trusted to have primary responsibility for discipline through its own procedures, and he urged tighter administrative control over faculty behavior.
3. Quality Controls. Critics of the academic occupation urged that modification of the format of a course without proper administrative authorization should not be permitted, that a teacher should be required to teach his or her course in reasonable conformity with the description announced in advance, and that the penalty for unapproved deviation should be an adverse performance rating.
4. Quantitative Controls. Some legislators suggested that advance notice of faculty absences from the campus should be required regardless of duration, with explicit administrative approval necessary for absences that exceeded a specified number of days; that classes must be held at times and in places officially scheduled; and

that each professor should be required to maintain a minimum schedule of office hours, with any deviation a cause for discipline. In Michigan, the legislature enacted a statute requiring full-time faculty members in the state's major institutions of higher education to teach ten classroom-hours a week, faculty members at other four-year institutions to teach a minimum of twelve hours, and junior college faculty members to teach a minimum of fifteen hours.

5. Personnel Administration. There were many attacks on faculty governance structures. One legislature deleted all monies in the budget for financing the activities of the academic senate of the university—later, and somewhat grudgingly, restoring less than half of the original amount, thus having made the point that governance structures live at the sufferance of the legislature. Ultimately, these threats went away, leaving no discernible mark on the academic occupation.

Two other recent efforts to regulate the academic occupation—one generated under the aegis of government and the other a species of direct government intervention—are worthy of note. The first is the establishment, where the faculty so chooses, of a collective bargaining system for determining the terms and conditions of employment either under the National Labor Relations Act in the case of privately funded colleges and universities or under state bargaining laws governing labor relations in the public sector. While collective bargaining systems involve private rule-making, they seldom arise in higher education in the absence of permissive legislation. Furthermore, they bring to life an entity external to the institution, an employee organization empowered by law to negotiate the terms and conditions of employment. In this sense, collective bargaining is akin to government regulation.

Collective bargaining caught hold in the middle sixties in elementary and secondary systems and in the latter part of the decade moved to higher education—community colleges, four-year colleges, and universities. The move to bargaining systems was particularly widespread in the public sector in states such as New York, Michigan, Wisconsin, New Jersey, Pennsylvania, Florida, and Minnesota. Growth was less marked in the private sector, but some privately employed faculties opted for collective bargaining. In 1976, there were 450 institutions of higher education engaged in collective bargaining, including 189 four-year colleges or universities, covering about 117,000 faculty members.

The other development is the national commitment, expressed in myriad laws and regulations, to prevent discrimination against minorities and females in hiring, promotion, and other aspects of the employment relation.

So far as can be seen, neither of these developments has yet made a substantial impact on the academic occupation. Collective bargaining has not demonstrated that it has the capacity to improve the economic lot of the professoriate,[2] and college and university administrations have in the main successfully prevented collective bargaining from meaningful intrusion into governance systems where they exist, or into institutional management generally. As for the status of women and minorities, there are neither significantly more members of minority groups and women now employed in the academic profession beyond the lower ranks than there were a few years ago, nor have they moved in large numbers into positions of authority in college and university administration, nor are their salary levels reaching toward those enjoyed by white males.

Nevertheless, it seems inevitable that as publicly funded higher education becomes more and more predominant and private institutions rely more and more on governmental largesse, there will be increased regulation by external agencies. Inasmuch as the uses to which public monies are put are constrained by constitutional and, more importantly, political considerations, there have been and probably will continue to be changes in admissions policies, program and curricula, student subsidies, methods for measuring student performance, and degree requirements, reflecting the widely held view that education is a service to be delivered in response to the demands of the marketplace.

But these changes are not solely the result of governmental pressures. They also reflect, as Sumberg points out elsewhere in this book, the understanding of institutional management that modifications are necessary in order to attract the new students essential for the stimulation of a new era of expansion. The work of members of the academic occupation, measured by values and performance, can be expected to be equally responsive to the social and political environment of the 1970s.

Similarly, women and minorities are likely to be the beneficiaries of changes in the profile of appointments, promotions, and tenure, although it is doubtful that the modifications will be dramatic. Obviously there have already been changes in the academic occupation. To some extent they have been the result of government regulation of higher education management. Thus, administrative decisions even where they do not literally constitute state action because the institution is privately financed may nonetheless take on that coloration where the monies that are expended derive from public sources. And in such circumstances, most members of the academic occupation enjoy increased constitutional protection against administrative actions which abridge protectable interests (for example, an expectation of continued employment) without due process of law.[3]

The bulk of the changes, however, are not primarily the result of governmental activity. They are largely a response to a changed environment, particularly the demographics of potential consumers, and a manifestation of institutional instincts for survival.

NOTES

1. A characteristic of institutions of higher education is the diffuse nature of decision-making. The University of California affords a good example of this phenomenon. At that nine-campus system there is a system-wide faculty council at the top of the governance structure. There are senates with an elaborate committee network on each campus, beneath which are the faculties of each college or school. Paralleling this governance structure is a management establishment consisting of central administration, deans, and department chairmen. The governance and management structures are connected by a skein of liaison arrangements. To identify who decides what is difficult, thus making it hard to bring a particular person to account and join an issue.

2. Where compensation levels for higher-education faculty have improved, it is not clear that collective bargaining is entitled to the credit.

3. 408 U.S. 564; 408 U.S. 593.

Chapter 9—Conclusion

The Peculiar Mixture: Public
Norms and Private Space

Stephen K. Bailey

In a generic sense, this book is trying to sort out what all generations of free people must sort out: that peculiar mixture of freedom and order that is compatible with evolving norms of social justice on the one hand, and with the fostering of both critical and creative impulses on the other. Government regulation of higher education is simply a subtheme of the eternal Yin and Yung of democratic politics: the need to promote equity without destroying individuality, the need to satisfy claims of fairness without stultifying essential life forces.

It is quite impossible to summarize adequately the textured richness of what has been presented in the foregoing pages. All that this concluding chapter will do is to abstract three themes that are of central importance as we face the future of government regulation of higher education.

Theme number one is perhaps best epitomized in a wise admonition of the late James Thurber: "Let us not look forward in fear, or backward in anger, but around in awareness."

Theme number two is that the essence of democracy is not in confrontation but in permeation; not in the adversarial proceeding itself, but in settling out of court; not in nonnegotiable demands, but (in a nonpejorative sense) in compromises and deals.

Theme number three is that, looking ahead, higher education will by and large get the kind of government regulation it deserves, or in Charles Saunders' felicitous phrase, "The next move is ours."[1]

On theme number one, the Thurber theme, let it be acknowledged that higher education vis-a-vis government regulation has frequently looked backward in anger or forward in fear. Faced with a largely novel sense of being crowded by government laws, regulations, inspections, and reports, many spokesmen for our colleges and universities have lashed out in irritation or foreboding. John Howard, president of Rockford College, believes that "affirmative action" is a large and fateful step "which the nation has taken toward intellectual and cultural suicide."[2] Derek Bok believes that government interference is the greatest single threat to Harvard's integrity in the years ahead.[3] Kingman Brewster has on occasion in recent years sounded like a latter-day Thomas Jefferson, fearing that the federal government is today's George III who, in the words of the Declaration of Independence, "has created a multitude of new offices, and sent hither swarms of officers to harass our people, and eat out their substance." Following Freudian laws of psychological displacement, other spokesmen in higher education associations and councils have ranted against the evils of government regulation, echoing E.B. White's lament that the world has gotten completely out of hand.

In retrospect, some of the concern—some of the shrillness—may have been justified; but much of it has not. Even if some laws and regulations seem unwarranted or carelessly constructed, it is useful to remember Macauley's insight that "reformers are compelled to legislate fast because bigots will not legislate early."[4] Many of the laws and regulations that trouble higher education have their origin in evidences of injustice, callousness, chicanery, and capriciousness throughout American life, as within the academy itself. We in this nation are undergoing a fateful revolution in regard to both substantive and procedural due process. This revolution is an attack upon inherited prejudice—what Lyndon Johnson called "unequal history"—and upon whimsical exercises of authority. The protections against these evils tend to find their embodiment in rules governing process. For those accustomed to the traditional decisional perquisites of station, the imposition of procedural constraints by outside authority is a pain in the neck. But as Justice Holmes once reminded us, "Liberty is secreted in the interstices of procedure." Procedure, to paraphrase an early hymnwriter, is "the bridle of colts untamed."

How many of us could honestly endorse a return to the days when, with impunity, college authorities could discriminate against Jews, or Blacks, or women in student admissions or in faculty hiring, firing, and promotion? Even today, in accordance with evolving norms of fairness and accountability, one cannot believe that most colleges and universities are adequately accessible to handicapped students, or that male and female staff are treated equally. Logically or politically, there is no sound reason why colleges should be excused from health and safety regulations and minimum-wage laws applicable to other populations and social institutions. And who can deny that some colleges and universities have permitted lax and sometimes fraudulent practices to occur in the allocation and expenditure of government grants or contracts?

As the distinguished Black educator, Charles S. Johnson, once wrote, "No one expects laws to reform the hearts of people; this is not their purpose. They can, however, and do, according to the venerable Judge Learned Hand, control the disorderly, even at times at the risk of making them angry."[5]

Colleges and universities are disorderly when they are capricious; when they discriminate on the basis of racial, religious, or sex prejudices; when they advertise in a misleading fashion; when they accept G.I. Bill money without some reasonable check on the attendance or academic progress of veterans; when they allow runaway grade inflation; when they execute budget transfers that violate government accounting requirements; when they maintain academic standards on the main campus but let them slide on a branch campus in a distant city or state.

This is not to suggest that such practices are universal, or that all of them are widespread. But their incidence is extensive enough to warrant deep public, and therefore governmental, concern. When Henry VIII, for reasons of personal convenience and lust, effected the Protestant Reformation in Tudor England, he enjoyed the support of a people suffused with an anticlericalism that had been building for centuries. If contemporary cries of anguish from the academy at being regulated by government are perceived by the general public to represent claims of immunity from the laws and norms of the larger polity, our academic abbeys will be no safer from destruction than were Glastonbury and Melrose.

An honest acknowledgement of the mote in higher education's own eye is a necessary part of the Thurberian notion of "looking around in awareness." We will not understand government regulation of higher education unless we understand why someone believes we deserve regulation.

But there is another aspect to our looking around in awareness. What is it that drives the government to be as inept as it is in fashioning and implementing the laws and regulations it writes? Surely few of the regulations governing higher education have been authored with clarity or enforced with efficiency. Part of higher education's wailing is the result of a signal ineptitude in legislative drafting and grotesqueness in the regulatory machinery. Picking out devils, of course, rids one of surplus adrenalin. We accuse congressmen of garnering votes by taking cheap shots at the academy. We conjure from the witches' brew of our anxieties a phantasmagoric montage of power-hungry bureaucrats, some of them disappointed academics, delighting in making us twist slowly in the wind. We watch government lawyers in their sullen trade, and accuse them of gloating as they spin their webs of red tape. Occasionally but not frequently our paranoia may conform to reality. There are kinder and more plausible explanations for the dysfunctions of the regulatory process.

First, many of the issues are exceedingly complex. There is nothing self-evident about how to be fair to everybody, or about how to catch real culprits without irritating the innocent. Government openness and individual privacy are both legitimate goals in a free society, but avoiding excruciating trade-offs in these interrelated fields is virtually impossible. When values and pressures conflict in the formulation of legislative policy threatening to wound the body politic, ambiguity is a standard analgesic. Those who lament the lack of clarity in legislative draftsmanship would frequently be outraged to the point of rebellion if legislative intent were in truth precise. Lawmaking is often the art of judicious obfuscation when clarity about values bitterly in contention would unduly rend the fabric of our community. There have been occasions (the Buckley amendment comes to mind) when higher education associations have been upset by the introduction of legislatively unconsidered items at ultimate points in the process.[6] But such instances are rare. The more frequent reason for what in retrospect turns out to be ambiguous or convoluted law is that the issues at stake are inherently complex and controversial.

Second, laws and especially those dealing with complex matters, are generally not self-defining. There is simply no way of writing general law so that its application to different realities can forestall injustice in particular cases. When the Interstate Commerce Commission was established in the late 1880s to set railroad rates, all Congress could do was to mandate that the rates be "fair and reasonable." An elaborate procedural machinery has evolved in this nation, as in other nations, to try to insure procedural due process in the application of general law to particular cases. The landmark study of the Attorney General's Committee on Administrative Procedures just before World War II,[7] ensuing legislation in 1946 and subsequently,[8] and various decisions by federal and state courts[9] have set basic criteria for procedural fairness. But the legal matrix is still evolving and those in federal departments and agencies charged with drawing up detailed regulations for carrying out legal mandates often find themselves caught in a series of contradictions or uncoagulated legal principles. There may be no way of making clear through regulations what Congress intentionally fudged in the law itself. Furthermore, if those who will be affected are to be involved early in the discussion of draft regulations to clarify and improve regulatory language, is there danger of collusion—of bringing the fox into the chicken coop? Secretary Weinberger thought there was such a danger and prohibited early consultations. Secretary Mathews discounted the danger and ordered his subordinates to consult early and often. Higher education associations have pleaded, with some success, for early openness in regulatory drafting. But most academic political scientists have certainly not been advocates of early openness in regulatory processes involving big business. A recent decision by a U.S. Court of Appeals for the D.C. Circuit appears to circumscribe early openness in regulation drafting, giving uncomfortable weight to the Weinberger doctrine.[10] In any case, the substance and the procedures of regulation-writing are neither obvious nor easy.

In the third place, *many* laws and agencies are often involved (and understandably so) in important areas of federal regulation. This is certainly true of the field of civil rights, equal opportunity, and affirmative action. But overlapping jurisdictions exist in other areas as well: the uses of humans and animals in academic research, occupational safety and health, academic fraud, auditing standards, and data requirements. One may rail against inefficiencies and duplication, and one may work toward simplification and consolidation.[11] But most of the overlap is a product of inadvertence and of honest efforts at bureaucratic compliance with legislative mandates, not of legislative or administrative venality. Moreover, it is not, alas, self-evident that the perceived interests of higher education are always better served by one powerful agency than by many weak and overlapping ones.

In sum, if we are to look around us with awareness, it is not helpful to search for willful devils. As Harold Laski reminded us decades ago, "Politics is . . . unintelligible if we simplify it to the point of making it the struggle of right against wrong, of good men against evil."[12] Once admitting this essential truth, we may be able to move to theme number two: the realization that the essence of democracy is in negotiation not in confrontation. Gellhorn and Boyer (Chapter 3) make this point with complete clarity. It need not be elaborated upon except to reinforce their contention that government regulation of higher education has been, on most matters and in most cases, an extraordinarily attenuated process of parry and thrust, give and take, threats and appeals, errors and correction, arrogance and contrition. One is frequently amazed at the variety of pressure points available to the higher education lobby when confronted with a threat from any quarter of the federal government: appeal to the good sense of the proximate perpetrator, appeal to his boss, appeal to the House, appeal to the Senate, appeal to the White House, appeal to the judiciary.

Not only do such appeals frequently temper the crusading fervor of individual bureaucratic zealots, they cause revisions of and adjustments in the system. Far from finding unfeeling bureaucrats or stubborn elected officials, higher education's representatives are constantly reminded of the permeability of the governmental membrane or, to change the metaphor, the willingness of the system to react positively to the "feedback loop" of informed criticism. In the past few years, higher education's associations and academic leaders have worked with a score of committees and commissions charged with improving some aspect or other of the regulatory process—an Interagency Task Force on Higher Education Burden Reduction, a Commission on Federal Paperwork, a Student Financial Assistance Study Group. There have been congressional efforts to help ease the regulatory burdens through provisions of the Education Amendments of 1976—administrative cost allowances, mandates for the coordination of federal-agency data gathering, mandated progress reports on paperwork reduction, conditions that regulations be promulgated not "as deemed appropriate," but "as may be necessary" (a subtle but important nuance).[13]

There is still much to be done. Roger Heyns of the American Council on Education recently outlined in a letter to President Carter a number of areas where, in higher education's estimation, the government needs to be more efficient and more prudent in the regulatory process: the coordination and administration of federal programs; the burden of new regulations imposed by the Veterans' Administration; overlapping jurisdictions in EEO, civil rights, and affirmative action; the need for "cognizant" (that is, lead) agencies in fields where many federal agencies now have jurisdiction; the removal of cost-sharing provisions in appropriations legislation; the raising of the minimum value of nonexpendable personal property that must be accounted for; adoption of the recommendations of the Commission on Federal Paperwork, especially as they apply to OSHA and ERISA reporting requirements.[14]

But what is significant about Heyns' letter is that it was requested by President Carter himself. And there are other examples of federal sensitivity. In the knotty area of overhead rates on federal contracts, Secretary Califano reacted immediately and positively to the suggestion made last February by a delegation from the higher education associations that the Undersecretary of Health, Education and Welfare, Hale Champion, review with a small academic task force a series of draft regulations drawn up within HEW last year governing indirect costs.

The daily work of ACEs Charles Saunders, Shelly Steinbach, Betty Pryor, and Laura Ford, and their counterparts in sister associations in identifying peril points of federal legislation, regulation, and judicial decision-making is an extraordinary success story not only because they are bright and energetic people, but also because we live in a democratic society in which government is responsive to intelligently developed petitions for redress of grievance. This does not mean that government is blameless. Nor is it always sensitive to the dangerous side-effects of well-meaning policies. Sometimes it is maddeningly slow or obtuse in discerning dangers in laws and regulations. But just as frequently it is responsive to anxious noises from those being regulated—sometimes to the point where those who should be benefiting have become cynical about the willingness of government to get tough. Witness the recent demonstrations of the handicapped in Secretary Califano's office protesting delays in the issuing of regulations. It would be easier, however, for the government to get tough more often if there were available graduated penalties that were less than apocalyptic. But such a degree of rationality in public policy is still ahead of us.

This brings us to the third and final theme—higher education by and large will get the kind of government regulation it deserves. This does not mean that, with the academy's assistance, government will always keep within the bounds of prudence and fair practice, or that it will always be sensitive to subtle differences in institutional needs and requirements. Again, to borrow from E.B. White, "The urge to solve a problem with a bulldozer or some other heavy piece of machinery is strong."[15] All of us need reminding that certain aspects of academic life can be regulated by the heavy machinery of government only at a fearful price. At this writing, the ACE is trying to fend off the heavy machinery of the Federal Trade Commission in various fields of advertising and fair practices—not because the academy is guiltless, but because there are perverse dangers in using an industry-oriented bulldozer to weed an academic garden.

Or consider the dilemma of eligibility and accreditation, posed on the one hand by the need of the government to determine which postsecondary institutions are eligible to receive federal grants, and on the other by the principle of academic quality control through private regional and professional accrediting agencies. If the U.S. Office of Education moves too far in its qualitative determination of eligibility, it usurps traditional accrediting functions and becomes a French ministry with power of life and death over our colleges and universities. Yet the Council on Postsecondary Accreditation—representing as it does the regional and professional accrediting associations of the academy—has neither the capacity nor the desire to move into the policing functions that would in essence make federal government inspectors of private accrediting associations. In this circumstance, where government criteria for determining eligibility leave off and private accreditation functions begin, the matter is one of continuing debate and uncertainty—especially when there is factored in the chartering and licensing role and responsibility of the several states.[16]

At the moment, what academics perceive as a government bull in the china shop is chasing what public officials perceive as an academic dog in the manger. Perhaps both sides must learn to appreciate that between detailed government accountability and complete institutional autonomy under private self-regulation is and must remain a no-man's-land or the general public may suffer. Neither government regulation nor self-regulation have been very efficient enterprises. As Edwin Neumann observed, "Since there always seem to be more inputs than outputs, there must be some 'puts' getting lost somewhere."[17]

None of this contradicts the central point of theme three: that is to say, the future of government regulation—its pervasiveness and its severity—will be greatly conditioned by what higher education itself determines to do about the issues enveloping it. If we in the academy do in fact look around with awareness; if we staff ourselves and our associations to bargain with government from a position of informational, analytical, and political strength; and, above all, if we demonstrate by our behavior that we can regulate ourselves in the public interest, the parade of terrors conjured by the term "government regulation" will largely disappear. The real question is whether we can learn to internalize John Gardner's precept: "Self-discipline is the yoke of free men."

The surest way to guarantee a continuation and extension of the kinds of government regulation we do not like is to play a self-righteous Thomas R. Becket to the Henry II of a pragmatic and popular government, to pretend that we are free from sin and that in any case government has no right to invade our bastions of sacred immunity even when we are unjust. Furthermore, if we are foolhardy enough to assume that higher education has more troops than the government in any direct confrontation, that we need not be sensitive to emerging norms of social justice, or need not attempt to put our own houses in order, then we will get what we deserve. The government will ultimately run us over, to the sound of applause from public bystanders.

There are test cases ahead, notably in the implementation of regulations governing the handicapped and, a little further along, in the carrying out of the Age Discrimination Act of 1975. Both of these new evidences of emerging social norms of equity and equality can be fought tooth and nail. Both can find higher education reacting like a cornered Tasmanian devil. But in both there is opportunity for higher education to internalize the new public norms and to prove by acts of creative response that it can anticipate and obviate the necessity for punitive regulations. Such responsiveness is not too late even in more traditional fields like affirmative action and occupational safety and health. But if academe does not react to government laws with more understanding and more creativity, it will find itself trapped in the dictum of Max Scheler. "True tragedy," he wrote, "arises when the idea of justice appears to be leading to the destruction of higher values."[18] Such a tragedy is both unnecessary and preventable. But the major burden of avoidance is on the academy.

This is not, however, to let government policy-makers, regulation-drafters, judges, and enforcement agents off the hook. They in turn must realize that not all of the injustices of the world are amenable to legal and administrative redress, that there are in fact legal and administrative therapies whose side effects are worse than the disease they were designed to cure. Society and the institutions that comprise it *can* be leveled to an equity that stifles rather than liberates. John Quincy Adams wrote in his *Memoirs* that the administrative age tends to be "an age of small men and things."[19] A society bound too tightly by tethers of litigiousness and pettifoggery can end up devoid of adventure—and without adventure, Whitehead noted, civilization is in full decay.

Government must be aware of the special financial burdens on colleges and universities that accompany compliance with new laws and regulations. Such costs have skyrocketed in the past decade, and colleges and universities find it difficult or impossible to pass these costs on to students in the form of higher tuition, or even on to hard-pressed state legislatures in the form of higher taxes. It is not unreasonable for higher education to request government assistance in meeting some of the administrative costs imposed by new government mandates. Higher education is still waiting for a full government understanding of, and adequate response to, this patently just request.

Over the course of the decades ahead, the long-range bargain between the academy and the government must be a trade of self-regulation for privacy. If those of us in higher education succeed in convincing the government that we are making an honest effort to keep ourselves aware of evolving norms of social justice, and are making these norms increasingly manifest within our own systems and institutions, then we may be taken seriously when we ask in return for some private space—space where odd and irreverent minds may ponder, create, explore, discover, criticize, nurture, transmit, and doubt, and where, in God's own time, both young and old, by unleashing the powers of the unfettered mind and the free spirit, may once again fill our fragile world with songs of hope.

NOTES

1. See Charles B. Saunders, Jr., "Easing the Burden of Federal Regulations: the Next Move Is Ours," *Educational Record* 57:4 (1973): 217–24.

2. Quoted in James Kilpatrick, "Congress and the Colleges," *Dallas Times-Herald*, March 14, 1977.

3. Harvard University, *The President's Report, 1974–1975*.

4. Thomas B. Macauley, *Speeches on Politics and Literature* (London: Everyman's, 1936), p. 53.

5. Quoted in Stephen K. Bailey, Howard Samuel, and Sidney Baldwin, *Government in America* (New York: Holt, 1957), p. 176.

6. Family Educational Rights and Privacy Act of 1974 (FERPA), P.L. 93-380, §513, *as amended by* P. L. 93-568, §2. For a useful review of "privacy" policy as it may affect higher education, see Sheldon Elliott Steinbach, "Employee Privacy, 1975: Concerns of College and University Administrators," *Educational Record* 57:1 (1976): 29–33.

7. "Report of Attorney General's Committee on Administrative Procedures" (1940).

8. 60 Stat. 237 (1946), *as amended by* 80 Stat. 378 (1966), *as amended by* 81 Stat. 54 (1967), 5 U.S.C. §§1001 *et seq.*

9. *Phelps Dodge Co. v. NLRB*, 313 U.S. 177, 61 S. Ct. 845, 85 L. Ed. 1271, 133 A.L.R. 1217 (1941). *SEC v. Chenery Corp.*, 318 U.S. 80, 63 S. Ct. 454, 87 L. Ed. 626 (1943).

10. *Home Box Office, Inc. v. F.C.C.* (March 25, 1977) (No. 75-1280).

11. See H.R. 3504, 95th Cong., 1st Sess., introduced by Congressmen Edwards (D-Cal.) and Drinan (D-Mass.). The Edwards-Drinan Bill would merge authority for administering several of the principal equal-opportunity statutes in the EEOC, and for the first time grant to that agency significant enforcement powers.

12. Harold J. Laski, *Where Do We Go From Here?* (New York: Viking, 1940), p. 20.

13. For a discussion of the work of these committees and commissions, and of congressional initiatives, see Saunders, op. cit.

14. Letter to President Carter from Roger W. Heyns, President, American Council on Education, March 25, 1977.

15. E.B. White, *The Points of My Compass* (New York: Harper & Row, 1962), p. 135.

16. Harold Orlans, *Letters from the East, the West, the North, the South, Private Accreditation and Public Eligibility* (Lexington, Mass.: D.C. Heath, Lexington Books, 1975). See also Kenneth Young, "Statement Presented to the Student Financial Assistance Study Group," Council on Postsecondary Accreditation, December 8, 1976.

17. Quoted by Morton Gerda, "Adult & Continuing Education," *Innovation* 8:2 [University of Michigan] (September 1976): 1.

18. Quoted in the Preface to Irving Hose, *Politics and the Novel* (New York: Horizon, 1957).

19. *Memoirs of John Quincy Adams* (Philadelphia: Lippincott, 1876), p. 117.

Index

Contributors

STEPHEN K. BAILEY is professor of education and social policies, Harvard Graduate School of Education.

BARRY B. BOYER is associate dean, Faculty of Law and Jurisprudence, State University of New York at Buffalo.

ESTELLE A. FISHBEIN is general counsel, The Johns Hopkins University.

ROBBEN W. FLEMING is president, The University of Michigan.

ERNEST GELLHORN is dean, Arizona State University of College of Law.

WALTER C. HOBBS is associate professor, Department of Higher Education, State University of New York at Buffalo.

ROBERT L. KETTER is president, State University of New York at Buffalo.

ALFRED D. SUMBERG is associate secretary and director of government relations, American Association of University Professors.

SHEILA TOBIAS is associate provost, Wesleyan University.

DONALD H. WOLLETT is director, New York State Office of Employee Relations.